The Complete Guide to

CHEER LEADING

All the Tips, Tricks, and Inspiration

The Complete Guide to

CHEER LEADING

All the Tips, Tricks, and Inspiration

CHRISTINE FARINA
and COURTNEY A. CLARK

MVP
BOOKS

Foreword by
CINDY VILLARREAL

Photography by
BRUCE CURTIS

First published in 2011 by MVP Books, an imprint of MBI Publishing Company and the Quayside Publishing Group, 400 First Avenue North, Suite 300, Minneapolis, MN 55401 USA

The information in this book is true and complete to the best of our knowledge. All recommendations are made without any guarantee on the part of the author or Publisher, who also disclaims any liability incurred in connection with the use of this data or specific details.

We recognize, further, that some words, model names, and designations mentioned herein are the property of the trademark holder. We use them for identification purposes only. This is not an official publication.

MVP Books titles are also available at discounts in bulk quantity for industrial or sales-promotional use. For details write to Special Sales Manager at Quayside Publishing Group, 400 First Avenue North, Suite 300, Minneapolis, MN 55401 USA.

To find out more about our books, visit us online at www.mvpbooks.com.

ISBN-13: 978-0-7603-3849-0

Library of Congress Cataloging-in-Publication Data

Clark, Courtney A., 1960-
 Complete guide to cheerleading : all the tips, tricks, and inspiration / Courtney A. Clark and Christine Farina ; with a foreword by Cindy Villarreal.
     p. cm.
 Includes index.
 ISBN 978-0-7603-3849-0 (flexibound)
 1. Cheerleading--Training. I. Farina, Christine. II. Title.
 LB3635.C6 2011
 791.6'4--dc22
                    2010052294

Editor: Adam Brunner
Design Manager: Brenda C. Canales
Layout Designer: Helena Shimizu
Cover designer: Sandra N. Salamony

Front Cover Photo Credit: Doug Murray/Icon SMI

Printed in China

TABLE OF CONTENTS

FOREWORD

WELCOME TO THE *Complete Guide to Cheerleading*!

Cheerleading has a dynamic history and a legacy of great leaders affording every aspiring athlete the opportunity to take part in the growing future. Being a cheerleader in today's world gives athletes the chance to learn, to grow, and to succeed. Cheerleading has become one of the fastest growing sports activities around the world. It challenges you to be a team ambassador, an exemplary student, a community service supporter, an athlete, a competitor, a fundraiser, and the list goes on and on. Not just for girls, cheerleading is coed and embodies true talent and athleticism. It also provides opportunities to be involved in many spin-off activities year-round.

Cindy Villarreal, former Dallas Cowboys cheerleader, featured on the cover of *Cheer Coach* Magazine.

What can be more special than to be part of a program that allows you to be in the limelight as a cheerleader and still participate in so many fun activities along the way? This opportunity is rare, and not many sports allow girls and boys the chance to be part of the same team. Cheerleading is for kids, schools, gym programs, sports teams, and special teams. Parents too are part of a niche group that performs in support of other teams. Cheerleading can be for anyone who wants it bad enough.

The Complete Guide to Cheerleading is the athlete's guide to preparing for the cheerleading lifestyle on and off the sidelines. This guide will benefit everyone from the beginning cheerleader to coaches and everyone in between. It is a must-read for anyone hoping to join the hard work, fun, and excitement of being part of a positive, growing legacy that is making a huge difference all over the world by empowering participants to be great in all they do. Leadership stays with you forever, and cheerleading can truly prepare you for life and lead to success in your later years. If you have willpower and self-discipline, you can accomplish your dream and be part of this exciting group of cheerleaders. Allow this book to be your stepping stone to making cheerleading a reality. Go out there and capture your dream!

A corporate cheerleader,
Cindy Villarreal
President, Proformance Sports Marketing
and Entertainment, Inc.
Agent, Cheer Channel, Inc.

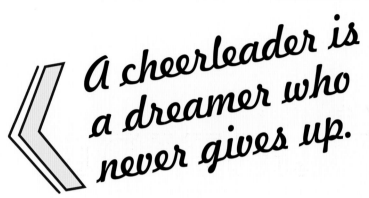

A cheerleader is a dreamer who never gives up.

THE HISTORY OF CHEERLEADING

CHAPTER **1**

CHEERLEADING IS A WELL-KNOWN and much-loved American tradition at sporting events. For 125 years, cheering has given us a variety of chants, cheers, and routines to motivate teams and excite crowds. Along the way, it has provided us with some great entertainment. Follow this timeline to see how cheering has evolved from simple crowd participation into a worldwide, competitive activity.

Shutterstock

1884

Exuberant crowds yell and scream to encourage their football teams. The first cheer is created at Princeton University.

1898

November 2, the birth of organized cheerleading. Tom Peebles brings the Princeton cheer to the University of Minnesota, where Johnny Campbell later becomes the very first cheerleader. "Rah, Rah, Rah! Ski-U-Mah, Hoo-Rah! Hoo-Rah! Varsity! Varsity! Varsity, Minn-E-So-Tah!" Johnny Campbell sure started something big!

Ivy League schools such as Yale and Princeton were some of cheerleading's earliest innovators. Megaphones and mascots are defining symbols of cheerleading throughout the world. *Terry Cook/Sports Illustrated/Getty Images*

1898–1899

A six-man group at the University of Minnesota becomes the first organized cheer squad. These "yell leaders" used Johnny Campbell's original cheer, still heard at Minnesota sporting events today.

Lawrence "Herkie" Herkimer

Lawrence Herkimer started running cheer camps in 1946. Fifty-two girls attended the first NCA camp in 1949. Today, Herkimer's camps boast annual attendance of over 20,000 cheerleaders. That's something to cheer about!

Unable to find a factory that would quickly manufacture uniform sweaters in the time between spring tryouts and the fall football season, Herkie purchased his own knitting mill for $100,000.

In a 1984 article in the *New York Times*, he said, "I have a plant that manufactures pompons. We have a knitting mill that knits the sweaters and a cut-and-sew factory that makes the jumpers and the blouses and the skirts."

That ubiquitous pleated skirt? The original was designed by his wife, Dorothy Herkimer!

Lawrence Herkimer demonstrates his eponymous jump, the "Herkie," which is still widely used today. Epitomizing spirit, the left leg is stretched forward in the toe-touch position, left hand on hip, and the right leg is bent behind, while the right arm punches straight up into the air. *Courtesy of National Cheerleader's Association*

Early 1900s

Used for public speaking since the 1600s, megaphones become a staple for all-male cheer squads.

A very enthusiastic male cheer squad leaps for joy along the sidelines of a University of Wisconsin football game. *Alfred Eisenstaedt/ Pix Inc./Time Life/Getty Images*

1923

Cheering is a natural fit when females first begin participating in collegiate athletics. The sport becomes more complex, incorporating gymnastics, pyramids, and throws, and has never looked back. Today, women represent over 97 percent of cheerleaders.

1930s

Pom-poms (now called pompons) are invented—an exciting addition to help squads stand out from the competition and add flare to their routines. Made of colored crepe paper, early pom-poms were great as long as the weather was dry.

1948

The National Cheerleaders Association (NCA) is formed by the grandfather of cheerleading, Lawrence "Herkie" Herkimer, also known as "Mr. Cheerleader."

1965

Organized cheerleading competitions begin nationwide, and rankings for "Top Ten College Cheerleading Squads" appear.

Fred Gastoff invents vinyl pompons. These vividly colored accessories hold up in the rain and snow, and are introduced into competitions by the International Cheerleading Foundation.

1967

The International Cheerleading Foundation (ICA) issues the first awards for "Cheerleader All-America." In 1995, the ICA reforms into the World Cheerleading Association (WCA).

Lawrence Herkimer created the spirit stick. Originally a consolation prize for an enthusiastic team who failed to win any competitions, it began as a branch broken from a nearby tree. The stick became a symbol for exceptional spirit. Soon red, white, and blue wooden batons were awarded to teams who displayed it. Legend says it is bad luck for the stick to touch the ground. Do you believe that?

1960s

National Football League (NFL) teams launch their own professional cheerleading squads. The Baltimore Colts is the first team to have its own cheer squad.

The inception of professional cheerleading brought a new level of excitement to the game with the Baltimore Colts sponsoring the first professional squad. *Paul Schutzer/Time Life Pictures/Getty Images*

1976

The Dallas Cowboys cheerleaders instantly become a household name with their televised appearance in Super Bowl X. Integrating revealing uniforms and skilled dance moves into their routines, the Cowboys cheerleaders changed cheerleading forever.

Cheerleading moves into other professional sports, most notably basketball.

The Dallas Cowboy Cheerleaders set the bar for professional cheerleading in the 1970s. *Hulton Archive/Getty Images*

Early 1980s

The start of the era of modern cheerleading. Cheering becomes a competitive activity, and competitive cheerleaders form All-Star teams.

2003

The National Council for Spirit Safety and Education (NCSSE) is formed to provide safety training for youth, school, All-Star, and college cheer coaches. All coaches must pass a certification program through either the AACCA or the NCSSE.

The Marlin Mermaids professional cheerleaders are the first squad in Major League Baseball and perform alongside the Florida Marlins.

2006

"Save the cheerleader, save the world" becomes a popular catchphrase from NBC's hit sci-fi TV series *Heroes*. Cheerleading is launched back into the pop culture spotlight by the show's main character, Claire, who exemplifies a positive image of high school cheerleading.

In late 2006, the U.S. All-Star Federation (USASF) further expands its reach by facilitating the creation of the International All-Star Federation (IASF), the first international governing body for the sport of cheerleading.

The Marlin Mermaids were the first cheerleading squad for an MLB baseball team. Since their arrival in 2003, a handful of other teams have added cheer squads as well. *Ronald C. Modra/Sports Imagery/Getty Images*

2007

Cheerleading and the game of cricket have their first international meeting at the International Cricket Council (ICC) Twenty20 Cricket World Cup in South Africa.

1983

ESPN first broadcasts the National High School Cheerleading Competition.

1987

The American Association of Cheerleading Coaches and Administrators (AACCA) is founded to develop and apply universal safety standards and regulate stunts used in routines.

Pennants are an old spirit tradition that continue to be popular with today's sports fans.

2000

The premier of *Bring It On*, a Hollywood film about a San Diego high school cheerleading squad called "The Toros," starring real-life former cheerleader Kirsten Dunst. Earning nearly $70 million domestically, it led to two direct-to-video sequels and remains a must-see movie for teens 10 years later.

2009

New rules for safety are implemented by the AACCA. These rules are included in Chapter 12's safety information.

Fox TV debuts the hit show *Glee*, in which cheerleading coach Sue Sylvester steals the show as a caricature of a hard-nosed, competitive coach who stops at nothing to win more trophies for her team, the "Cheerios."

The Future

There has been much talk about competitive cheering becoming an Olympic sport. In preparation for that day, an American team awaits the opportunity to shine on the world stage.

Don't be a Sue! FOX's hit series *Glee* may be a bit over the top when it comes to depicting the head coach of the Cheerios— but she's certainly entertaining! © Fox Broadcasting/Patrick Ecclesine/Photofest

Famous Former Cheerleaders

RUTH BADER GINSBERG

Born in Brooklyn, New York, Ruth Bader Ginsberg cheered at James Madison High School, went on to study law, and served as a professor at Rutgers University School of Law and Columbia Law School. After serving 13 years as a federal judge, she was appointed to the U.S. Supreme Court by President Bill Clinton in 1993. She was only the second woman to hold this position, and the first Jewish woman to do so.

KATIE COURIC

Well loved for her upbeat demeanor, Katie Couric cheered for Yorktown High in Arlington, Virginia. As a journalist, she worked at CNN and as a Pentagon correspondent for NBC News. Her combination of perky and smart led to 15 successful years of incisive interviews as co-anchor of NBC's *Today Show*. She made history in 2006 when she joined CBS News as the first woman to be a solo evening news anchor.

PAULA ABDUL

A California girl with honor roll credentials, Paula Abdul first cheered at Van Nuys High School and later was a squad member and choreographer for the famed Laker Girls while attending California State University. A hugely successful choreographer, dancer, and singer, this multi-talented dynamo even created a DVD cheerleading exercise series entitled *Cardio Cheer* in 2005. She became a household name for her role as a judge on *American Idol*, and she continues to push the creative envelope with her own collection of jewelry designs and fragrance.

Paula Abdul received the Laker Girl award in 1991, and Hall of Fame basketball legend Magic Johnson joined her on stage to present her with her framed purple uniform. *Anna Maria DiSanto/WireImage via Getty Images*

Cheerleaders Who became United States Presidents

GEORGE W. BUSH
President No. 43 cheered at Phillips Academy in Andover, Massachusetts, before dabbling in oil drilling, professional baseball team management, and finally politics.

RONALD REAGAN
President No. 40 cheered at Eureka College in Illinois before going on to a Hollywood film career and then politics as governor of California prior to his presidency.

DWIGHT D. EISENHOWER
President No. 34 was an all-around athlete and cheerleader at West Point Academy in New York before rallying U.S. troops and their Allies to integrate land, air, and sea operations in World War II.

FRANKLIN D. ROOSEVELT
President No. 32 cheered football at Harvard University before his political career. As president, he cheered up the entire nation with the New Deal after the Great Depression.

CHEERLEADERS — Bush, Booth, Sartore, Brown, Greene, Cowen, Townend, Franchot, Gonzalez.

George W. Bush showed his spirit as a cheerleader for his high school, Phillips Academy in Andover, Massachusetts. *Copy photo by Darren McCollester/Newsmaker/Getty Images*

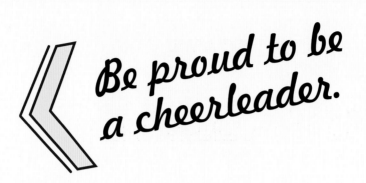

Be proud to be a cheerleader.

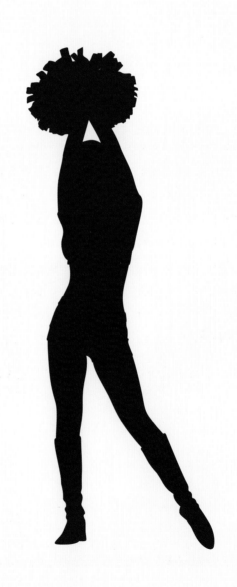

TYPES OF CHEERLEADING

CHEERLEADING HAS COME A long way since the early days of all-male yell teams. Today there are many opportunities to become involved in cheerleading based on your interests, talents, and commitment level. You may simply want the experience of representing your school and enjoying cheering. You may have the goal of one day becoming a professional cheerleader for an NFL or National Basketball Association (NBA) team. You might be hoping to represent the United States in international competitions, or even in the Olympic Games. This chapter will review these opportunities to help you decide which type of cheering would be the most fulfilling for you.

School-Sponsored

Beginning in middle school and progressing through high school and college, students can join cheerleading squads to promote school spirit and motivate players and other students. While school-sponsored squads primarily cheer for sporting events and encourage audience participation, some also participate in local, regional, or national competitions.

Unlike most seasonal school-sponsored programs, many schools offer the opportunity to participate in year-round cheer-related activities. Tryouts for the following year are held each spring or at end of summer for football season, and some schools hold separate tryouts for basketball season. There are organized camps and team practices during the summer, and cheering at sporting events and competitions takes place in the fall and winter.

MIDDLE SCHOOL

Middle school is such an exciting time of growth, development, and self-discovery. What better way to participate in the new social environment of middle school than to represent your school as a cheerleader, spreading spirit and excitement?

Cheering in middle school consists of sideline cheering and half-time performances at football and basketball games in the fall and winter, as well as performing at school pep rallies. There may be opportunities for competition as well. You'll follow the same rules and regulations as high school squads when it comes to safety issues and the types of moves allowed on the sideline and in performances. These new rules are printed in their entirety in Chapter 12 on safety.

Performing is all part of the fun in middle school cheerleading. *iStockphoto*

HIGH SCHOOL

Although similar to middle school, high school cheer squads definitely take it up a notch in terms of participation and competition. Some larger schools have two squads, a varsity squad for the more advanced cheerleaders and a junior varsity (JV) squad for the less experienced. Some schools also have a freshman squad. While these teams are largely determined by grade, it's common for both JV and varsity squads to have participants of all grades based on ability.

Bringing spirit to the school is the primary responsibility of a high school cheerleader. In addition to sideline cheering at football, basketball, and sometimes wrestling and other sporting events, half-time performances, pumping the crowd up, and encouraging audience enthusiasm, you will also be a key participant in fundraising activities and pep rallies. This participation includes making posters to display in the school to announce rallies and games.

If you want to become involved in the competitive aspects of cheering, many schools have squads that compete at the regional, state, and national levels. This type of cheering makes *you* the athlete. Due to the nature of competition with stunts and tosses, these squads are coed more often than non-competitive squads are.

COLLEGE

While college squads may be coed, many all-girl squads still remain. Depending on the size of the school, there may be more than one team. One team may perform solely on the sideline, at games, and in pep rallies, while the other team focuses on competitive cheering. At a smaller school, these teams may be integrated and will focus on game routines early in the season and competitive routines during the year. Some college cheerleaders receive athletic scholarships to participate on cheer squads that compete nationally and internationally.

Regulation stunts become more challenging and technically difficult at the collegiate level. Stunts may include flipping skills, 2 1/2 high pyramids, and flipping and twisting basket tosses. Practice times vary from two hours daily to only three or four times a week.

High school cheerleaders will learn to perform stunts together.

Cheering from Coast to Coast

David Kirschner, The Spirit Consultants, LLC

While cheering is as American as apple pie, there are regional differences in how we cheer across the United States. At high school football games on the East Coast, cheerleaders face the bleachers with the goal of getting the crowd involved with the cheering. On the West Coast, cheerleaders face the field and stand on boxes so that they can see above the crowd and cheer the players.

In addition to the cheer team and the dance team—which doesn't cheer, wears its own uniforms, and perform half-time shows—many West Coast squads have an additional squad of song leaders. This group wears the same uniform as the cheer squad and will cheer and use pompons. The difference is that song leaders don't stunt. While the cheerleaders may build a stunt to celebrate a touchdown, the song leaders will do kicks or pirouettes. Song leaders may even compete against other schools in their own competitive divisions.

Pep rallies vary greatly from school to school based on the creative input of individuals, but how they are organized can be a regional difference. In many parts of the country, pep rallies are created and run by the cheer squads. In some areas, a group called the Associated Student Body (ASB), which is similar to Student Council and is a partnership between the school and student leaders, will be in charge of the pep rallies and will allocate time for the cheerleaders during the rally. And while warmer weather states like to have their rallies outdoors on the field or the quad, northern states opt for indoor venues like the gymnasium.

Cheering on a college squad is a big honor—and a big responsibility. As a college cheerleader, you may receive national exposure at marquee sporting events, and your team will have an opportunity to compete at a high level. Left: *Victor DeColongon/Getty Images* Center: *Ronald Martinez/Getty Images*

Youth League/Athletic Association

Sports leagues in many communities are sponsored not by schools but by local leagues and associations. They frequently use school district facilities or those of the local town. Many of these organizations sponsor football and basketball leagues, and many also sponsor cheerleading squads to cheer at their events.

Two organizations that have many chapters across the country are Pop Warner and Young Men's Christian Association (YMCA). Pop Warner has been around for 50 years and is the largest youth football and cheer/dance organization in the world. Its mission is to help young people participate in organized sports and cheer activities in a safe and structured environment while teaching fundamental skills and values that will be used throughout their lives. As part of its life skills philosophy, Pop Warner requires participants to maintain adequate grades in school. Its cheer program operates year-round and offers novice, intermediate, and advanced squads. YMCA programs offer the opportunity for girls ages 5 through 12 to learn cheering basics and test them out at YMCA-sponsored sporting and camp events.

All-Star

Cheering that is not affiliated with a school or sports league and is dedicated to competitive cheering as a sport is called All-Star. Independent gyms across the country are devoted to training all-girl and coed teams of between six

Gabrielle, age 16

There are a lot of differences between school and All-Star cheering. With school cheering, you have to be more mellow than with All-Star, and you have to act more mature. With All-Star, you can be kind of fun and crazy. There are certain facials you can do in All-Star that you can't really use in school. All-Star you can wear a half top and show your stomach, whereas at school you have to be more clean-cut. Even with the makeup, you can't wear so much. With All-Star, you can go crazy with your makeup and hair.

I definitely like to do this facial during All-Star [mouth open wide with arms up]; sometimes they think it's too showy. I like blowing a kiss or something, or like doing a shimmy. I love to shimmy. I like to land and pop up and do one of these [shimmies]. Or do a "you-call-me move." You land your tumbling pass and you do "You" [points to crowd], "Call" (holds hand like phone up to ear), "Me" [points to herself]. And you walk away. It's a lot of fun, but you can't do that in school because they would be, like, "What are you doing?"

The most fun about being a cheerleader is definitely in bonding with the team; you get so close with them during the season. You get to hang out with the girls so much you become a family with them. I just love hanging out with them.

Gabrielle cheers for her high school squad and on an All-Star team.

and thirty-six athletes for regional, national, and international competition. Some, but not all, participants also cheer for their school squads.

All-Star cheering is a year-round activity, and teams generally participate in eight to twelve competitions each year. Of course, this varies based on the gym, the number of competitions won (winning allows a team to advance to the next level), and travel funds available. Local competitions often take place in school gymnasiums, while regional and national competitions are typically held in larger convention center venues. HP Field House in Orlando, Florida (formerly Disney's Wide World of Sports Milk House Complex), hosts the cheerleading world competition. Routines for these competitions are 2 1/2 minutes long and are choreographed to music with precise timing and synchronized stunts, tumbling, jumping, and dancing.

Most All-Star participants have taken gymnastics and dance classes. The age range is broad, from 5 to 18 years and older, and participants are classified by several divisions: Tiny, Mini, Youth, Junior, Junior International, Junior Coed, Senior, Senior Coed, Open International, and Open. There are also many different levels within these divisions.

The All-Star Division began in the 1980s and, due to various gyms vying for titles without a coordinated system of rules, was initially unregulated. In 2003, the USASF was formed as the national governing body to standardize rules and judging criteria. In 2004, cheerleading coaches formed a similar alliance called the National All-Star Cheerleading Coaches Congress (NACCC), which then joined the USASF. The USASF finally went on to become the International All-Star Federation (IASF), the first international governing body for the sport of cheerleading dedicated to the safety of cheerleaders.

Professional

Professional cheerleaders combine dance abilities with some gymnastics. While some organizations are currently adding stunts to their routines, we can expect professional cheerleaders to be more skilled in all aspects of cheerleading in the future. Football cheering is geared toward large motions and the use of pompons to fill the huge space of the field, while basketball cheering requires tighter, more choreographed dance moves that work in the smaller space of the hard court. As representatives of teams that invest millions of dollars in branding, professional cheerleaders require strict observation of the rules of etiquette, dress, and behavior. Professional sports are big business and proper presentation is vital to their success. Professional cheerleaders may receive opportunities for acting, modeling, and other off-the-field/court representation, which adds to the excitement and glamour of this prestigious position. Like their younger, school-based counterparts, professional cheerleaders wear their uniforms proudly while performing numerous community service activities.

All-Star Cheerleading

Competitive cheering is the goal for All-Star squads. The chance to excel, bond with your teammates, and have loads of fun ensures everyone's a winner.

National

We may see cheering as an Olympic sport one day soon, and there is currently a national team through USA Cheer and the USA Federation for Sport Cheering. This team represents the United States and is composed of select cheerleaders, over the age of 18, from teams across the country. The team competes against 130 other national teams from 60 nations around the world. The future of cheerleading is definitely global!

Summer Camps

Whether they be sleep-away or commuter day camps, cheer camps are often hosted by a cheer organization or a local college or university. Sometimes entire cheer squads go to camp together, and college-level cheerleaders often team up in a buddy system with high school teams for instruction. Camp days are filled with cheer-related activities, including warm-ups, jumps, dance routines, learning new cheers, and performing new stunts. Because there is so much concentrated cheer activity, teams can really improve in a short period of time.

Cheer camp is not all about skills and routines. One of the most popular benefits of camp is the bonding between teammates and the opportunity to make friends with cheerleaders from other schools.

"The thing I love most about cheer camp is the bonding with my team. Hanging out with the team is the most fun ever. I love my team. I also love dancing. I love learning dances and practicing them over and over again like crazy. Cheer camp is 24/7 cheerleading. You know what I'm saying? You're always doing something. I love it!"

- Gabrielle, age 16

Many young cheerleaders struggle with embarrassment and issues related to peer teasing. Getting away to a camp environment is the best way to overcome these feelings. At camp, no one will think you're being silly for going in front of a large group and being loud and smiley. Instead, you will be surrounded by peers who value your enthusiasm and share your feeling that the cheesier the performance, *the more crowd effective*. After bonding as a group with your squad mates and other cheer groups, and really letting it all out in your performances, you'll find it easier to go home with plenty of confidence in what you and your squad are doing.

"I like the camp experience because I love meeting new people. When we see them at competitions, we can bond with them and do routines and wish them good luck."
      - *Spenser, age 14*

"The camp experience is great. I can get so much training for these stunts, and I really like the way the college team buddy system helps us out."

- Carly, age 14

"What I like about the camp experience is the staff; they're very out-going. They are here to teach us and make us better, and we'll take everything we've learned and make it our own and just succeed from it."

- Ivette, age 17

Enthusiasm runs wild at cheer camps and memories that will last a lifetime are made right here.

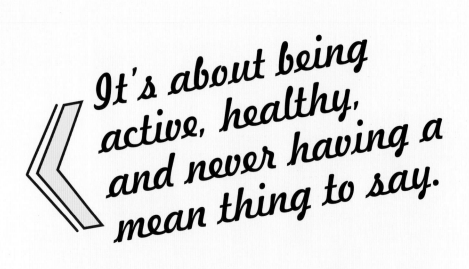

It's about being active, healthy, and never having a mean thing to say.

WHY BECOME A CHEERLEADER?

CHAPTER 3

THERE ARE MANY REASONS to cheer, but eight-year-old Victoria, who has already been cheering for over two years, does a great job expressing one of the most important reasons: "It's really fun!"

And she's right. Let's look at some of the reasons why.

Do you have someone that you look up to in your life, perhaps a cousin, an older sibling, or even an Olympic athlete whom you've watched in competition? What about that person do you admire? Do you enjoy his or her positive attitude toward life and other people? Do you admire his or her self-confidence? Maybe you're in awe of that person's determination to reach goals. Think about the type of person *you* want to be, and imagine the traits you would have. Cheerleading can help you bring together many positive attributes to become the person you really want to be.

Shutterstock

Positive Attitude

A cheerleader is the personification of positive attitude. Look no further than the name itself. If you look up "cheer" in the dictionary, you'll find plenty of positive:

1. a shout of joy used to urge on, welcome, approve, congratulate
2. a state of gladness or joy
3. anything that makes one happy; encouragement
4. to become gladsome or joyous
5. to dispel gloom, sorrow, or apathy from; to fill with joy, good spirits, and hope; gladden

But how do you acquire the ability to be the embodiment of cheer? Some people seem as if they are born with it, but everyone struggles to overcome obstacles of some sort. You'll never have a trouble-free life, but the secret is to rise above your challenges and disappointments and to keep going. *And that is all about attitude.* There is an old saying that if you're feeling down, you should force a smile and a laugh, and before you know it, you'll feel better. There is truth to this. Try it next time you're feeling blue. Instead of wallowing in your mood, seek out a family member to say something nice to (give an unexpected compliment!), call a friend and have her tell you a joke and make you laugh, or do an unexpected favor for someone else. When you turn your attention outward, you will find it impossible to remain stuck in your mood. Your problems or struggles may still be with you, but you won't allow them to control you.

With a positive attitude, almost *anything* is possible. Few things are accomplished well without the desire to put everything you've got into the task. Having a positive attitude will help you with your schoolwork, because you will look at the tasks as opportunities to do your very best, not simply a pile of must-dos. A positive attitude will help you develop and keep friendships, because it is enjoyable to be around someone who offers a smile. Since part of a positive attitude is about looking outside yourself, your friends will appreciate that they have your attention and understanding when they need it.

Cheerleaders display their positive attitudes with smiles and stunts while having fun.

Developing a positive attitude becomes even more important as you grow into adulthood. Employers want people who are eager to work and can rally everyone around a task. While it only takes one person to sour the mood of an entire office, the converse is also true. One person who is happy to handle whatever comes her way is worth her weight in gold and can make a great impact. *Never underestimate the power of being positive.* Not only will you find you can achieve more, you will also help others achieve more.

Francesca, age 15

I've always liked tumbling, but there was no gymnastics team at my school. I joined the cheer team because gymnastics is part of it. I love being part of an actual team. Gymnastics is more of an individual sport, and I love the dependence and trust you get from cheering. Plus, everyone's really nice.

My non-cheer friends were very supportive of me going out for cheerleading and were really happy for me when I made the team. A great thing about cheerleading is that it brings people from different groups together. I like walking through the halls and saying hi to people from all different groups. It makes me feel that I know everyone and that this is truly my school.

Cheering has taught me determination because we work so hard. It has also helped me to be outgoing and more confident. It's not easy when a stunt or new routine is not working, but I just keep saying, "Next time will be better; it's not the end of the world." I take cheering seriously, but I don't get devastated if we don't win or something goes wrong. I don't take it to heart because I know there will be better days.

My favorite moment in cheering is when you finally master a stunt you've been working on or a new skill on the mat. Competition is a real adrenaline rush!

Off the field, cheering has helped me with my time management. Sometimes when I come home, I just want to crash and not do my homework. Knowing that I've got cheer practice to go to helps me get it done more quickly. Because I have a lot of practice time, I know I can't leave things until the last minute anymore like I used to. Knowing that I am busy helps me to get school projects finished earlier.

Cheering has also helped with social skills. I haven't had any problems with other members of the team, but it is really important to keep problems outside. If you have a problem you can't resolve, you definitely need to take it to your coach. The other girls on the team may not be my best friends, but being part of a team has taught me how to get along with others. I've learned that you don't have to hang out with people to get along with them.

And, you can't let yourself be embarrassed. You just have to make a joke of everything that might get in the way of you going out there and doing your best cheering.

Francesca has combined her love of gymnastics with her love of cheering.

"I was so shy when I first entered middle school that I was afraid to make eye contact with anyone and hid behind my long hair. I really wanted to be a cheerleader though. After I made the team, my shyness just kind of went away and people couldn't believe that the outgoing me was ever shy."

— *Susie*

Self-Confidence

Most young girls struggle to gain self-confidence; if you find yourself in this situation, you are not alone. Lack of self-confidence and shyness can hold you back from reaching your potential and experiencing life to its fullest. Cheering can help by providing a safety net of team members to back you up as you grow and develop your confidence. And because there is safety in numbers, you will gain more self-assurance as you work together.

Only YOU can change yourself! Cheering won't change you, but it's a great vehicle for bringing out the very best in you and allowing your own natural and beautiful personality to shine through. Cheering sets standards of both personal and educational achievement within the community, and humans have a wonderful capacity to rise to the occasion. When high standards are set, you will have goals to live up to. After that, it's about discovering who you are and achieving your very own personal best as you naturally grow into this role.

Great posture with shoulders back and head held high shows that you have confidence in yourself.

"The most important parts of being a cheerleader are to be positive and to be responsible. Cheerleading teaches responsibility because you are in charge of equipment and things which must be done or your team won't be able to compete."

— *Stephanie*

Determination

Determination, like self-confidence and positive attitude, may seem to come more naturally to some— but there is a key. The key to determination is finding a goal that is meaningful to you. There is an old maxim that says, "If you love what you do for a living, then you will never have to work a day in your life." If you apply positive attitude and a love of what you are doing to any activity, you will find that determination is automatic. It may still be hard to get out of bed on a cold winter's morning to train before school, but you will find you want to get up more than you want to stay in bed, because the desire to achieve is burning inside you. Any athlete, no matter how gifted, has to train hard and build his or her life around a sport. You may need to schedule time to accommodate training, games, and competitions, or keep a regimented diet to maintain optimal fitness. While from the outside this looks like intense determination, a dedicated athlete is simply doing what he or she needs to in order to continue down the path toward success.

The only way to master a new skill—like this "collegiate pyramid"— is to keep trying and that is what determination is all about.

Friendship

Experiences are best when they are shared with friends, and being part of a group of friends with a common purpose can be very rewarding. Cheerleading requires you to work together through difficult practices and lost games and allows you to share cherished moments of victory or accomplishment, such as landing a new stunt. Cheerleaders need to rely on each other during stunts and thus need to develop mutual respect and trust. When people relate to each other, friendship often follows. Many girls feel that the friendships they develop through cheering are the best part of the sport.

If cheering is what you love, then give it your heart and soul. It will repay you by instilling self-confidence and determination, and by giving you standards and goals to live up to while you enjoy every step of the way.

Cheering together on a squad helps develop trusting friendships; which is a winning combination.

"A good cheerleader is a responsible person. You need to be a leader and present yourself well . . . We learn from our coaches and from camp all the things that are expected of a cheerleader, and it is up to us to behave that way."

— *Jillian*

The Cheerleader's Creed

- Be prompt
- Be patient
- Be polite
- Be loyal
- Be truthful

- Be compassionate
- Be friendly
- Be determined
- Be a team player
- Be a good student

- Be interested in the world
- Be tolerant of others
- Be constructive, not critical
- Be positive

What Makes a Good Cheerleader

From a coach's point of view, a good cheerleader is one who is *coachable*. Most coaches take on the job out of passion for the sport and a desire to teach and support the girls on the squad. What makes the experience worthwhile is having a team that wants to be there as much as the coach does. Here are a few ways to make the most of your opportunities to be coached.

Listen to your coach. This means paying attention when the coach is talking and not whispering to a friend or daydreaming about your upcoming weekend plans or all the homework that must be done. You are there to cheer, so get your head in the game. Listening is not just a courtesy; it's also a safety issue. You need to pay attention to instructions so you don't make a mistake that might result in injury to yourself or others on your squad. You can show that you are listening by being attentive and by making any changes in your skills that have been suggested.

Be *open-minded* about trying new things. Your coach will push you in order to challenge you and take your skills to the next level, so trust that your coach has the right judgment. Even if you're hesitant about a change in the routine or afraid to attempt a new stunt, push through the reluctance and give new things a try. Know that your coach has your best interests at heart and is pushing for you to achieve your own personal best.

Learn to take constructive criticism. We'd all love to hear that everything we do is great, but the bottom line is that we all have room for improvement in everything that we do. Don't become defensive if your coach offers some suggestions or requests

"I think a good cheerleader is a well-rounded athlete, someone who can cheer, dance, stunt, and tumble."
- Nicole DiSalvo

What Coaches Look For

Matt Jones, assistant coach and former cheerleader for Hofstra University, New York

Who do I want on my team? I look for someone who is engaging and fun to be around—someone who has good energy and charisma, is outgoing, responsible, and has a good head on their shoulders.

I *don't* want someone who thinks they know better than the coach, won't take constructive criticism, and won't make the time commitment to do all the extras, like community involvement, that make up an amazing squad and really make a difference.

Initiative and bringing your own ideas are definite pluses. I love it when kids do their own research by watching other teams on YouTube, creating new chants, and generally bringing new ideas in. We may not use them all, but the enthusiasm and thought behind it motivates me and everyone else on the team to push ourselves to be the best we can be. So go that extra mile—it will be noticed and appreciated!

that you make changes in your performance. Instead, appreciate that you have someone to give you guidance and direction.

Fostering a *positive attitude* at practice will make a more rewarding and fun experience for everyone, including yourself. Remember, very few things get accomplished in life through negative actions or attitude. It's all right to be hard on yourself, but you must be able to work through it. *Positivity is the key to success.*

Have good *energy* at practices. You'll get a lot more accomplished by keeping your energy up. Be sure to get enough sleep, eat healthfully, and keep your stress levels down. If you are feeling tired or run down, try taking some deep breaths and exhale slowly. Deep breathing will revive your body with oxygen and make you feel more alert.

Lead a *well-rounded and well-balanced life*. Time management is very important. Not only will it free you up to focus on the moment (a requirement when stunting), but it will alleviate the stress of school, homework, and activities. A major component of time management is not procrastinating. The longer a task is left undone, the bigger and more difficult it will seem to be. Frequently, once you've tackled a project that you've been avoiding, you'll find yourself saying, "This isn't so bad."

Being a good cheerleader is synonymous with being a *good role model*. What other people see and often want to emulate about cheerleaders is their enthusiasm. Your enthusiasm should not be left on the gym floor either. A spirited involvement in your community will reflect well on you, your coach, and your school.

A Guy's View

David Kirschner, The Spirit Consultants, LLC

I've played football, basketball, and other sports and think that, hands down, cheerleading is the most challenging sport there is. I think it is also the most rewarding sport that a male athlete could ever do, because it helped me to grow in so many ways. I became more confident socially, had my self-esteem boosted, and generally became more well rounded. I learned some valuable life lessons as well. For example, the college team that I cheered for was not the highest ranked team but would have 50,000 fans come to the games. As the underdog, I felt that I was in a sales position and my job was to market my team to the fans. I learned how to sell, and I got comfortable with public speaking by interacting with the crowd—two great skills for the job market.

A Cheerleader's Lifestyle

SCHOOL CHEERLEADING

Cheerleading is about more than having an upbeat attitude and performing in front of a crowd. Achievement in any sport or activity requires commitment and consistent work to further your goals. Your day-to-day activities as a cheerleader will depend on whether you are a school cheerleader, an All-Star, or both.

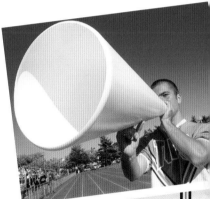

Glenn Kubalko/ Getty Images

ROLE MODEL

As a school cheerleader, your primary responsibility is to represent your school every day by providing school spirit. As a school representative, it is an honor and a privilege to stand for the very best that the school offers. You should always be striving for your personal best, in both your actions and academics. While having a moral code may sound daunting, it simply means that you should try to be friendly, kind, and thoughtful in all situations and to encourage others by your example. Just as a cheerleader on the sidelines of the game leads the crowd with her positive energy, your positive attitude throughout the rest of your day should also inspire others to emulate, or copy, your infectious upbeat style. When you smile, the world smiles with you, so never underestimate the power of a smile or a kind word. And remember that your actions don't just reflect on you, they reflect on your school. Representing your school doesn't end when the school day does; you will be recognized throughout your community because of your high visibility at school functions. The attributes of a cheerleader must become yours for all aspects of your life. *Enjoy* being an important part of your school community every day.

PRACTICE AND GAMES

You will have after-school practice three to five times per week lasting two to three hours each, depending on your school and your coach's schedule. Activities at practice will vary,7 depending on whether you are preparing for an upcoming game or a competition.

In addition to practice, you will be showing your stuff at afternoon and evening games. Junior high and high school cheerleaders will cheer primarily for football and basketball. If you are not already familiar with the basic rules of these sports, you should take the time to learn them. You can ask a sibling, a friend at school, a member of the team, or a coach to go over the basics with you. You'll want to know the difference between offense and defense and some basic plays so you can cheer confidently. You'll also enjoy the game more if you know what is going on.

Remember that you represent positive attitude! Even if your team is down or a referee makes a bad call and the crowd is booing, it's your job to pick them up and give encouragement. *Never* boo along with a crowd. *Always* keep smiling. Throughout the history of sports, many games have been won

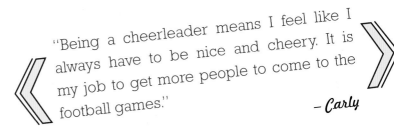

"Being a cheerleader means I feel like I always have to be nice and cheery. It is my job to get more people to come to the football games."

— Carly

in the final seconds when victory seemed impossible. These amazing come-from-behind wins happen when teams stay focused and continue to play hard (or harder) until the buzzer sounds or the whistle blows. Of course, it doesn't always result in victory, but that's OK—you are encouraging a positive attitude!

Halftime is your time to shine, and you will move from the sidelines to center stage to perform a routine. In middle school/junior high, your coach will usually select the songs and develop choreography for the team. In high school, this job may fall to the team captain. Developing a routine is a creative activity that can be fun as well as challenging. If you are learning a routine that a teammate has created, be encouraging and complimentary. If there are parts that you feel don't work as well as others, try not to be critical. Instead, start with a compliment, such as, "I really like the beginning skill, but I'm finding it hard to change to the next skill. Could we try doing it like this instead?" People generally find it difficult to hear criticism and can get defensive or angry. By starting out with something positive, you are putting your teammate in the right frame of mind to listen. By giving a suggestion, you are showing that you care and are a part of the team. If your suggestion is turned down, don't get upset. If your attitude shows that you are willing to be part of the team and to help out, your teammate will be asking for your advice before you know it.

All-Star Cheerleading

There are different levels of All-Star cheering, and your level will make a difference to your lifestyle. Some girls represent their schools for sideline cheering and also represent the best of their schools for a gym doing competitive cheer. Others may only do All-Star cheering. Each coach sets his or her regulations as to whether or not you will be allowed to participate in both school and All-Star. You will need to check with the school cheer coach and the local cheer gym to find out the rules.

When cheering for a gym, you can expect to have practices a maximum of three times a week. During the competition season (typically November though May), you will have events almost every weekend. Even as a beginner, you will travel throughout your state and to other states in your region. As you progress, you can expect to travel even farther.

When you are a competitive cheerleader, your practices do not stop with cheering. You may also need to take outside classes in gymnastics and dance, both integral skills to today's cheer routines. Additional preparation for this athletic activity will include regular exercises to increase flexibility for jumps and stunting, as well as overall conditioning to build the strength and energy necessary to withstand a two-and-a-half-minute routine.

Living the life of a cheerleader means balancing practices, games, competitions, school, and family. Achieving this balance can be challenging, but with a positive attitude and some help from your parents, teachers, and coaches, it's a challenge you can meet. So put on your game face and get out there!

A high school cheer squad shows off an arabesque stunt on a beautiful day.

"My favorite things about cheerleading are the Nationals, traveling, competing, and camp. I like making up routines too."

- Jillian

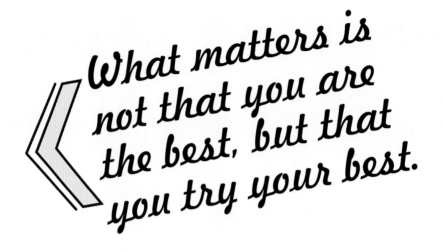

What matters is not that you are the best, but that you try your best.

DOING YOUR PART

CHAPTER 4

TO LIVE THE LIFE of a cheerleader is to inspire others by example. Your enthusiasm at games and pep rallies will spread through the stands to help make an enthusiastic crowd. Your positive attitude about your school and fellow students can spread throughout the school and help others to feel proud. Your charitable activities will inspire your community because you will be working toward a better life for all as a shining beacon for the future. In this chapter, we will look at some of the things cheerleaders do to inspire others in their schools, squads, and communities. We'll also look at some fundraising ideas to help make it all happen.

Shutterstock

"School spirit is what gets me up every single morning to go to school. I think that cheerleading, academics, and school clubs are about looking to our future. It's what we're here for, and it helps us become better people every single day."

- Marissa, age 16

In Your School

Other than the actual act of cheering, keeping up school spirit and getting turnout for the games are the most visible parts of cheerleading. Your tactics for revving everyone up are limited only by your *imagination*. The key to a great pep rally is to get everyone involved. Enlist your teachers to learn cheers and do cartwheels to surprise everyone. Get the guys on the football team to try cheering and stunts, and if they're game, maybe dress them up as a rival team's cheerleaders! Initiate new coaches with a fun prank (think whipped-cream-pie-in-the-face-type humor). The more you can surprise your audience and make them laugh, the more into it they will be. Search "pep rallies" online for dozens of fun ideas to borrow or use as a springboard for your own creativity. The end result should be a sense of shared experience, unity, and *fun*.

"Every year I come back because I'm just in love with it. I'm in love with the team, the coaches, everyone supporting each other."
- Amanda, age 17

In Your Squad

Cheer squads often start to feel like families, as girls and their coaches share the triumphs and tribulations of cheering, as well as those of life in general. Being a good team member and doing your part means treating others with the respect and caring that you would like to receive.

Don't ever badmouth others on the team. If you have a difference of opinion or don't feel that a teammate is behaving appropriately, try seeing things from her point of view before you judge. If you need to talk it through with someone to get to a point of acceptance, consult your coach about it privately so you can vent in a safe way that won't create bad feelings among the team.

Have each other's backs. If you overhear remarks about another girl on the team, don't join in any teasing or laughing; stand up for her. You both wear the same uniform and you are on the same team, so look out for each other as you would for a sister.

Turning Tragedy into Positivity

The Sachem North cheer team had a very meaningful season when one of its members, who was a junior at the time, was diagnosed with lymphoma. It was a scary time for the girl and for the whole squad, as they had never dealt with life-threatening illness before. In addition to being very supportive of its teammate, the cheer team turned its anxieties into action. The team held a Relay for Life race with over 80 participants to raise money for cancer awareness.

Building on the success of the race, the coaches organized a Pay it Forward scavenger hunt that started with the team making a trip to the hospital's pediatric cancer ward, where the cheerleaders buddied up with the young patients. They were each given $10 and a clue that led them to a local Target store where they shopped for their buddy. The next clue led them to an Applebee's restaurant where the coaches sponsored a dinner while the team members wrapped their purchases. They all returned to Stonybrook Hospital and presented the gifts during a holiday party.

Later on, the girls went Christmas caroling through the neighborhood and raised an additional $300 donation for the hospital.

The cheerleaders learned that tragedy can beget positivity, and the story has a happy ending. The girl with lymphoma made a complete recovery and was able to compete at Nationals that year—where Sachem won. She is now studying to be a teacher.

Make each other feel special. Be sure to celebrate more than just the obvious things like birthdays; take advantage of other opportunities to let your teammates know how much they mean to you. Did a teammate perform well in a band recital? Did she become a big sister? Was she in a school play? People feel special when you make the effort to know more about them and their lives.

Be there for support in the hard times. True friends don't shrink away when times get difficult. It may feel uncomfortable to deal with tragic situations such as death or illness, but providing comfort to a friend in need is truly a gift.

"My fondest memory [of cheering] is just being with the whole team, acting like the family we are, and just having a great time. I will really miss that."

- Ivette, age 17

Cheering and the Peace Corps

Laura Vaughn, Austin, Texas

In rural Ecuador, the Peace Corps conducted a sociology study that demonstrated the importance of after-school activities for kids. In poor areas where the school districts could not afford organized clubs and sports teams, kids were quitting school and falling into struggles with drugs and teen pregnancy. The Peace Corps' mission was to implement sports programs for kids through donations of supplies, uniforms, and coaching. While the sports programs worked well at keeping the boys in school and out of trouble, they did not have the same success with the girls.

One of the Peace Corps volunteers came up with the idea that cheerleading might be a more interesting activity for the girls and contacted Proformance Sports Marketing and Entertainment in Austin, Texas, for help implementing the idea. Cindy Villarreal, the president of the company, was very excited to help this project bring cheerleading to a broader audience. Proformance began a donation campaign for uniforms, shoes, hair products, and accessories. They also held a contest for a volunteer coach. Squads from all over the United States had the opportunity to participate in nominating their coach as "the Cheer Ambassador to Ecuador!" The winning coach spent time in Ecuador teaching the basics of cheering, stunts, and gymnastics to the newly formed squad. The contest culminated with the team cheering on the sidelines at a soccer game played by teams also set up by the Peace Corps.

The hope is that the squad will continue and grow though grassroots efforts, and that this could eventually be a pilot program for the Peace Corps worldwide. Whether or not the project ever reaches that level of success, one guarantee is that some very lucky girls have had the experience of a lifetime!

"We do a lot of charity work that is brought to the team by the coaches or captain. We raised money to shop at Target and made baskets for underprivileged kids. We also participate in breast cancer awareness walks. I don't like having to get up really early in the morning for the walks, but it is for a good cause and we do it as a team."

— *Francesca*

In Your Community

They say that to give is better than to receive, and it feels so good when you do things for others. When people talk about the volunteer work or community activities that they are involved in, what typically comes across is the notion that the person helping out actually feels to have gained more from the experience than the person whom has been aided. Humans are wired by nature to function in a group, and we feel good when we contribute our part. We also are born with an instinct to help others, and when we focus outside ourselves and put our energy into the world around us, it is an incredibly satisfying and fulfilling experience.

Cheering can give you opportunities to reach outside yourself and enjoy the benefits of giving. Most cheer squads participate in local charity walk-a-thons, community outreach programs, and telethons, while some squads are casting a wider net and finding ways to contribute to the global community.

In addition to upholding the name of your school and providing you with a sense of purpose and belonging, expanding the world of people that you encounter and interact with can lead to new opportunities that may give direction to your life.

Cheer for Joy and Shooting Stars

THE FIRST AND ONLY SPECIAL NEEDS CHEERLEADING TEAMS IN THE LONG ISLAND, NY, AREA

Coach Marissa Hillebrand of Gravity Cheer

Members of the Shooting Stars learn some basic stunts.

I was inspired to create this program when attending an out-of-state All-Star competition. There with my team to compete, I remember sitting in the stands when the announcer asked for a warm welcome for the special needs team about to take the stage. I was working toward my special education degree at the time and had always had a special place in my heart for children faced with disabilities, so this really got my attention. I watched the team's performance in amazement! I was also amazed by the crowd's rousing reaction to this team. As the performance came to an end, the music stopped, and the cheerleaders hit their last motion—I couldn't help but fight back the tears. I said to myself and my family that day that I would start a special needs team.

After a lot of research and time, the Cheer for Joy special needs cheerleading team was up and running in April 2009. We have a total of 11 participants in the program, 7 of whom are on the competition squad called Shooting Stars, and we're still growing. We meet once a week for an hour and are joined by All-Star cheerleaders, local school cheerleaders, and family members in coaching these athletes on the physical and social aspects of cheering. While each team has a different focus, we work with both groups on functioning as a team. Teambuilding helps kids build socialization skills, establishes appropriate group behaviors, instills self-confidence, and forges new friendships.

The Cheer for Joy team is for participants, who we call "Stars," who choose not to perform or compete but seek to learn the fundamentals of cheerleading and participate in our fitness program. We take the athletes through a variety of activities, such as obstacle courses, tumbling, and track games, that focus on building and stretching muscles to develop strength, flexibility, balance, and coordination while improving fine and gross motor skills and overall conditioning.

Shooting Stars is our performance/competition team. Their sessions focus on routines and choreography, tumbling, stunting, and the fundamentals of cheerleading. We are able to tailor the program and the routine to the needs of each Star.

We have many goals, including performing at a number of events around Long Island. We plan to show support for athletes during the Special Olympics, join the All-Star team at a Long Island Ducks minor league baseball game, and exhibit at regional All-Star competitions. My dream is to compete at Hershey Park at the end of every season.

But Cheer for Joy and Shooting Stars are about so much more than goals and performances. By giving everyone the opportunity to be a part of the wonderful world of cheerleading, we focus on *abilities*, not *disabilities*. I couldn't do it without the amazing volunteer coaches who come in every week with an eagerness to coach and an incredible sense of excitement when the kids learn something new or accomplish something they've been working on. It is such a positive experience for us *all*. We end each practice with a high five and a smile and, more often than not, a hug too!

Cheering is as much about spreading joy and helping others as it is about achieving your own personal goals.

Fundraising

Raising money is part of most clubs and activities, and cheering is no exception. Going to competitions is very expensive—it can cost $2,500 per girl to go to Nationals! Here are some favorite fundraising ideas. The internet is a treasure trove of additional ideas for raising money.

- Door-to-door selling with product catalogs like Dippin' Dots ice cream, Mary Kay cosmetics, and cheesecake.
- Car washes.
- Athletic clothing sales; sweats and tees with custom artwork and designs.
- Cheerleader for a Day event; twice a year, the squad hosts a day to teach cheering basics to elementary school girls. This type of event can draw between 40 and 120 attendees, and you charge in the neighborhood of $25 each. A popular time for this event is the week before Christmas, as parents can drop kids off at the event while they do their holiday shopping.
- Cheerleading competition: Host a local competition for teams in your area before a Regional or National competition. Hire professional, qualified judges so teams can receive feedback on their performance. Participating teams and spectators pay entrance fees to cover costs and raise money.
- Journal: In conjunction with hosting a cheerleading competition, squad members can solicit advertising from local merchants at $125 per full-page ad. The 30- to 40-page ad books are printed and given away at the competition, with as much as 70 percent of the revenue going to the cheer squad.

These fundraising activities could not be accomplished without a lot of help from parents. Cheerleaders' parents sometimes form their own groups, often called Booster Clubs, to help coaches coordinate events and will sometimes even design and order athletic clothing and accessories to be sold. Parent groups also coordinate with the school's parent–teacher association (PTA) and other school-based fundraising groups to ensure there are no overlapping events or efforts.

Fundraising can be more fun when you all work together; a shared goal means shared success.

 "We do car washes and bake sales. I love doing them because it helps us bond as a team. Also, I love baking and bringing in cookies."

– Carly

I don't cheer;
I inspire.

INSPIRATION

INSPIRATION COMES FROM MANY places in many ways. But the impact of that one moment that takes your breath away—or gives you a great idea, or encourages you to try something new—can last a lifetime. Cheerleading can invoke many inspirational moments because inspiration is what cheering is all about. Cheerleaders push players to perform their best on the field, encourage the crowd to add to the excitement, and put their best feet forward in their schools and communities to set examples for others. Cheerleaders also inspire each other. In this chapter, cheerleaders and coaches share their thoughts on how they were inspired to be cheerleaders and why cheerleading inspires them.

Shutterstock

My Story

Lenée Passiglia, Hofstra University

Every little girl wants to be *something* when she grows up. Some want to be a doctor, or an actress, or a lawyer. I wanted to be a cheerleader. I'd never given much thought to the kinds of accomplishments that cheerleading would bring into my life. When I began as a middle school cheerleader, I was nothing more than a small girl with big dreams, trying something new. I wasn't always sure of myself, but the more I cheered the clearer my vision became: I wanted to be a cheerleader for a lot longer than just my time in high school. Cheerleading was not just an after-school activity for me; it was a release, a place I could go to work hard to achieve the goals I'd set for myself. By tenth grade, I already had my mind made up: I was going to cheer in college, and I was going to cheer for Hofstra University.

It is difficult for me to picture my life without my Hofstra cheer family. I have been through the best and worst times with these talented individuals, and throughout the course of my four years on the team I have made lifelong friends and learned the best lessons anyone could ever teach me. I achieved many cheer accomplishments while in high school, including team MVP and Long Island All-Star, as well as being the captain of my varsity team the very first year we won the regional competition and went to UCA Nationals. But it's safe to say that my most outstanding triumphs came as a result of being a Hofstra cheerleader. In 2006, we won UCA College Nationals and went on to win titles in 2007, 2009, and 2010. Also in 2007, I was selected to be one of *Inside Cheerleading* magazine's Collegiate All-Americans. Five years, four championship rings, and an All-American honor—because of

Lenée Passiglia was *American Cheerleader* magazine's Cheerleader of the Month in December 2008.

Hofstra, I am in a very elite group. Some college athletes compete all four years without even a single taste of what it's like to be a champion.

I've come a long way from the somewhat-less-than-confident girl who had doubts and fears and speculations about doing big things. With the love and support of my family, teammates, and coaches, I've achieved goals I never thought possible. My most recent accomplishment is more like a dream come true. I was selected out of a large group of girls across the country to be the December 2008 cover girl of *American Cheerleader* magazine, thanks to my coach's encouragement. You see, with a heart full of dreams and a confident outlook, I have been able to make a name for myself in the cheerleading world. I am proud to say that I have overcome my insecurities and apprehensions, and if I could give one piece of advice it would be to always have a new goal to reach. Don't ever settle for being second-rate, because cheerleading calls for a first-place attitude. With dedication and drive you can do anything, and even the smallest dreams can make a great impact on your life. Be proud to be a cheerleader! I'm living proof that anything is possible with hard work and whole lot of faith.

"My favorite day was the first time I ever competed on an All-Star mat. Just getting my hair and makeup done, I got so excited and had butterflies in my stomach. I was anxious because I didn't know what to expect at all. I walked into the arena and saw all the lights and all the cheerleaders—it was such a great feeling. Right before we went on the mat I got all nervous and tense, but then once we got out there we just knew what to do."

- Gabrielle, age 16

"I do skating, tumbling, and dance as well as cheering, and my mom has to schedule it all! I love competing and think that the best advice is to stay calm and don't think too much about it so your nerves don't get to you. My greatest moment was when I finally did a lib. It took a lot of hard work to achieve, so I felt so great!"
- Alex, age 12

Paige, age 15

I started out as a gymnast, but I liked to watch the cheer competitions on TV. I got a charge out of the gasps in the crowd when they do the flips in the air and I think that is what inspired me to cheer. My teammates have become my best friends and I trust them absolutely. Because you need to know that your teammates will be there to catch you, this trust is physically important; but I think you also get emotional trust that bonds you together as friends for life. Conflicts happen because you are working closely together with so many other girls. But it is not safe to let emotions get buried or fester. I've learned how to confront issues with others and work them out so that we can perform with confidence. This is a skill I've learned from cheering that I can use beyond just with my squad.

Paige has been to cheer camp at the University of Maryland and has practiced gymnastics for nine years.

"I've been cheering since I was in first grade and my favorite thing is to pump up the crowd and have them respond to the cheers. But cheering has helped me to learn that it's not all about me. I've learned how to work with others and see what we can all do together."
- Julianna, age 13

Carly, age 14

I want to be an actress one day, because I love entertaining people. I tried out for the cheerleading squad in my first year of high school because it was a way to get out in front of the crowds and entertain, which is a big change from the cross-country running I did in middle school. Since I'm just starting out, the most challenging stunt I've done so far is the star pyramid, but I look forward to accomplishing a big stunt like a basket or a lib.

Carly enjoyed cheering with local youth athletic leagues when she started out.

Nicole, age 13

There is a lot of work involved in learning the cheers, and you really learn a lot about trusting your teammates because the stunts can be scary. When kids tease me about being a cheerleader, I just tell them, 'Wait for the game!' Once they see us out there performing our stunts, I know they'll see what it's all about.

People think that cheerleading is a simple sport, but when you get on the team you realize it's a lot more than waving your arms and screaming.

Victoria, Alexandra, and Christine

I knew I wanted to be a cheerleader when I first saw girls doing flips and stunts at a football game. I loved the aerial flips, and when I heard everyone say, 'Wow! Look at her,' I knew I wanted to have them say that about me. My training is in dance, gymnastics, and sports and I love being able to combine all my skills into one sport. One day I want to be a professional cheerleader, but I have a lot of work to do before I'm ready for that. In the meantime my goal is simple: Have fun cheering!

- Victoria, age 8

I've been doing gymnastics and going to cheer camp for four years, and cheering really helps me to feel good about myself. If you're afraid of what your friends will say if you try out for cheerleading, my advice is to say go for it!

- Alexandra, age 8

I'm on three cheer teams so there isn't much time for anything else with school and homework, but I don't even mind because most of my friends are on the teams. I've had to figure out how to be really organized with my school binders and work, which has taught me a lot about responsibility. Sometimes when I'm having trouble learning a stunt, I give myself faith by telling myself that I *really want it*.

- Christine, age 12

**Victoria and her friends Alexandra and Christine
look forward to spending time together and cheering together.**

Your Coach and You

A coach can be a guide, a mentor, a strong shoulder to lean on in tough times, and an overall inspiration to the squad. Whatever role is played, one thing is for sure: You will never forget this relationship.

Amanda, age 17

Two years ago, my team started off the season really badly; we were struggling in the beginning and by December we wanted to quit. Then January came and the coach said, 'New year, fresh start; we got this, let's do this.' We put our heads together and we just knew we could do it. It was like our love skyrocketed and we joined together and we actually won third place at competition.

Amanda's experience has taught her that the bond between teammates can make all the difference.

"My coach is an unbelievable woman, and I can't even begin to explain the many things she's done for us girls. She gives her heart and soul, her blood and sweat, and though it sounds corny, she is a teacher that has done more than teach. She's been as much of a life coach to any of us as she has been a cheer coach. I can't thank her enough for it."

- Marissa, age 16

Coach's View

Jamie D'Andrea, a fifth-grade elementary school teacher who started cheering in junior high and **Elizabeth Schlitt**, a high school chemistry teacher who started cheering at age 8, are now coaches for an award-winning squad.

They both cheered in college and jumped at the chance to coach when their school asked for volunteers. Their schedules are busy—they coach varsity and junior varsity together and trade off being the head coach between fall and winter seasons. Practices are five days a week from July through March, with a game or competition on the sixth day. April, May, and June are occupied with tryouts, car washes, and other fundraising activities. The coaches' involvement does not end with the season. Jamie and Elizabeth even get involved in the futures of their cheerleaders by sending requests out to colleges to assist in getting placements and scholarships.

These coaches put their all into the squad and require the same in return. All girls must sign a code of conduct as a requirement of participation. Agreement to treat the team and the coaches as family is vital to the mutual support and monitoring that Jamie and Elizabeth feel is necessary for trust and safety. If girls are on Facebook, they must be friends with the Sachem site so that the coaches can monitor all their online activity.

They say that "girls are often surprised at how involved we are in their lives. They think that we are crazy sometimes, but they also realize that our lives revolve around them and they love us for it. We preach positivity about everything from coaching to teamwork."

Another part of the code stresses the importance of social situations within the squad. The girls are told from day one that there can be no fighting within the squad. Arguments can be dangerous when a team must trust each other absolutely. While girls may not be the best of friends outside practice, coaches insist they learn how to separate those feelings and leave them at the door. The competitiveness and the desire to win, or do a great routine, help the girls to leave animosities outside. This is a great life lesson: Wherever you might find yourself, you know you have the ability to get along with others to accomplish something.

Learning to work as a team can be very rewarding, and even the coaches can be pleasantly surprised at how effectively their squad developed this talent. Teamwork can become second nature, and even if you are not in the competition group, you should keep your head in the game as you never know when your time will come. Here is a story that illustrates this point beautifully: During a competition, one girl injured herself just as the squad was about to build a pyramid. An alternate who was on the side with a banner saw what happened and quickly jumped in to take the place of her fallen teammate. Despite a quick switch in the middle of the routine, they had a perfect score and took first place!

 "We have a tradition before each competition where the coach gives us the words to a song printed out. She plays the music while we all sing the song together. It is a lot of fun and gets us relaxed yet full of energy to go into the competition."

- Jackie

"The cheer coach noticed that I was a bit lost after my father died. She encouraged me to try out for cheerleading because she figured it would be a new experience for me and would get me involved in something to help me move on. It was a very good decision. Having the support of the team and the coach helped me to figure things out. The coach helps us in so many ways. She's very strict, but it's a good thing because she always wants us to do better and wants the best for us. We had a great season and won the Long Island Champions, and it really meant a lot to me."

— *Ivette, age* 17

Cheerleaders work diligently with their coaches to perfect their routines. Your coach will be the leader of your squad and a positive influence in your life. *Kevin P Casey/ Bloomberg via Getty Images*

From Weak Link to National Champion

Dustin Santoni knows a lot about hard work and dedication to cheering. A gymnast when he was younger, he decided to try out for cheerleading at the age of 14. Like many guys, Dustin was motivated to try out the new sport for a simple reason: He wanted to meet girls. He made the squad, but he was always in the back of the formation because he couldn't lift, jump, or keep time. Admittedly, he was the worst in the pack. Embarrassed by his lack of skills, he stepped up his commitment to practices and ending up falling in love with cheering. By the end of high school he was in it to win it and became a team leader.

Early on, Dustin set his sights on getting a national championship ring. He knew he wasn't blessed with natural talents but felt that he could overcome that with a lot of hard work and practice. He cheered for Arizona State University but really wanted to represent the University of Kentucky, so he made up a résumé video and sent it off. He was invited for tryouts, and when he looked around at his competition he saw a lot of talent. An honest self-assessment told him that his skills were middle-of-the-pack, and that he would really have to work hard to impress the judges. He did and he made the team, although he was sore for days from trying so hard.

Joining this 14-time national champion team was almost a dream come true. Dustin still wanted a championship under his own belt. Fortunately, his new band of brothers all felt the same way, and he credits the entire team's "amazing, unstoppable attitude, talent, and work ethic" for making it finally happen. Along the way, the team developed some shorthand for the mentality that helped it get there. It included thoughts such as "We will not drop," "Throws should look so easy that anyone could do them," and "We should be so solid in our lifts that it would be like growing roots into the floor."

Dustin went on to cheer at the University of Hawaii and is now a coach himself. He sees cheerleading as a great opportunity to travel the country and see the world, but mostly he admires how it makes people happy and how a really great routine can literally make people's mouths drop in awe.

 TIP: Matt Jones, Hofstra assistant coach, likes to organize group activities to keep everyone motivated throughout the year. Scavenger hunts build unity, challenging ropes courses help build trust, and Halloween parties where everyone dresses as another member of the squad promote a silly way to appreciate each other.

What I Learned From Being an Assistant Coach

By Brienne Heiberger

I started cheering when I was 2 years old! Cheerleading means the world to me and is all I talk about. It is my favorite thing because it combines a fun sport with lots of close friends. I love stunting and the rollercoaster of thrills that comes with competition; the nerves that build up to it, and then getting on the floor and letting all that nervous energy out!

I'm in eighth grade now and, in addition to cheering on my school squad, I work as an assistant coach for the fourth-grade girls. Cheering is so different from a coach's perspective! I realize how much more important safety is than I thought. I've learned how to do each of the different spotting positions, how to tighten up the counts, and how to catch the girl right away and not have anyone get smacked in the face. *Safety is the number-one priority.*

Another lesson was that by paying attention to the coach you will not only be safer but can learn a lot more and do a lot better. I see now that the coach is not only concerned about individual performances but is also focused on the bigger picture. Everything counts in competition, and certain stunts will earn more points than others. The coach has to consider whether the team can safely perform the more challenging routines.

My experience as an assistant coach has made me a better member of my school squad. I definitely pay more attention to my coach and try to encourage the other members of my team by setting the example of what I wanted to see from the girls I coached.

Coaching is something special, and I hope to cheer in college and be a coach myself one day. The relationships that I've had with my coaches are really special. They are like best friends—I feel comfortable with them, can tell them anything, and they understand me and my abilities. I hope to be that special person for a team when I am older. I never want to leave cheering out of my life!

Twisting through the air, this cheerleader must trust that her teammates will be there to receive her safely into their arms—that's what teamwork is all about!

High Flyers

What could be more inspirational than literally flying high? These photos of high flyers exemplify how cheering can help you reach new heights. Remember: The sky's the limit!

To win or lose, the difference is one—one goal, one point, one extra mile of effort.

CHAPTER 6

GETTING READY FOR TRYOUTS

GETTING THROUGH TRYOUTS IS your first step toward being a cheerleader. You will be more confident and perform at your best if you are prepared and know what to expect. The first question to ask yourself is, "Should I try out?" You need to consider all that goes into being a cheerleader.

It is best to speak with your parents and get their approval. They will be responsible for driving you to practices and games, so they need to agree to spend the time to do that. A junior varsity team usually has two practices a week plus games. A varsity team may have up to four practices a week plus games and travel.

Next, you should consider your academics. Are your grades where they should be, and will you be able to maintain them while taking on extra activities? While cheering can be beneficial to your life in many ways, you don't want your schoolwork to suffer because of it.

You will also want to consider your personal reasons for becoming a cheerleader. Do you truly enjoy cheerleading and want to represent your school, or do you just want to wear the uniform around school? Be honest with yourself! You are making a commitment that involves a lot of your time and energy, as well as the time and energy of your parents and coach, so be sure that you are doing it for the right reasons.

Once you have made the decision to go for it, get ready to give the best that you have.

Preparation

First, you'll need to find out the "when, where, who, and what" of the tryouts.

WHEN

Tryout times vary depending on the school. Find out from the school if your tryouts are in the spring before school ends, in the summer before school starts, or in September when school starts.

WHERE

You'll need to know where they are taking place. Usually tryouts are at the school or in a local community center.

WHO

Find out whether you'll be performing in front of just the coach or if more people will participate in the decision-making. Having this information will help you mentally prepare for the tryout.

WHAT

Find out who the coach is and ask about the expectations and requirements for jumps, tumbles, and stunts. Generally, tryouts consist of individual skills, group routines, and an interview. If there is a constitution (a guideline for being a member of the squad), be sure to get a copy and review it thoroughly.

Sample Tryout Skills Sheet and Scorecard

GYMNASTIC SKILLS Execution, Difficulty		/10 points
JUMPS Toes Pointed, Flexibility, Height		/10 points
COMMUNICATION SKILLS Voice, Facial Expressions, Confidence		/10 points
MOTION TECHNIQUE Sharp Motions, Strong Motion Placement		/10 points
DANCE TECHNIQUE		/10 points
STUNTS Technique, Execution		/10 points
APPEARANCE		/5 points
OVERALL IMPRESSION		/10 points
JUDGE'S TOTAL		/75 possible

A positive attitude and genuine smile will help you shine at tryouts.

Once you've found out the basics, it is time to start working on your skills and to practice, practice, *practice*. Use a mirror to evaluate yourself when practicing. If you are new to the sport, your best resource is to talk to people first.

Ask the coach if you have questions. Be sure to take notes so you can refer back to them as you prepare. Ask girls who have been on the team previously to help you learn the jumps and stunts and motion placement, such as the high V or the low V. Seek out a gymnastics center to help you learn skills such as cartwheels, somersaults, and back handsprings, if you don't already know them. Putting in the extra effort will really help you to stand out. But you will only stand out in a good way if you are honest with yourself and the coach. If the judge asks you if you can perform a back handspring at the tryout and you have never tried one before or cannot do one successfully, just say, "No, but I'm working on it." *Do not* attempt to perform moves that you are not comfortable with.

If you have already been a cheerleader and are trying out again, you still need to put in effort. The coach will be looking to see that you are trying to improve and get to the next level. So brush up on your old skills, make sure your positions are sharp, and try to conquer a new tumbling skill.

In addition to skills, there is usually an interview portion of the tryouts. The coach will want to know what you feel your personal strengths are and what you will bring to the team in terms of positive attitude, confidence, and enthusiasm. He or she will ask you about your personal goals and why you want to cheer and represent your school. It is a good idea to think about your answers and practice them aloud ahead of time to help you sound self-assured and thoughtful.

During the interview, be honest and keep your answers focused on how you can make a positive impact on others and your school. Some answers that are *not* going to win you points are those that seem overly self-centered, such as:

"I think I'd look good in the uniform."

"I want to be popular and looked up to."

"I want the boys to like me."

Better answers would be:

"I'd be so proud to wear the uniform and represent the school."

"I'd like be a good role model for others."

"I am enthusiastic about sports and competition, and would love a way to show my support for the teams."

Be sure that your responses show enthusiasm for both yourself and your school, but always put the school first.

At the Tryout

Have you ever heard the expression "you only get one chance to make a first impression"? Your appearance will be the first thing the coach notices, so make sure to put some thought into it.

- Show your school spirit by wearing your school colors somewhere, either in your shorts and top or a hair ribbon.
- Dress in form-fitting clothes. Baggy clothes don't look as neat and can minimize the sharpness of your movements. Additionally, baggy clothing can be a hazard during stunts if a hand or foot becomes stuck in the loose fabric.
- Your overall appearance should be neat, meaning clean clothes with no holes or frays, and clean hair kept off your face.
- Wearing a small amount of makeup is ok as a way of accentuating your expressions, but go *light*. Heavy makeup can send the wrong message, so it's better to appear a little washed out than to look overly made-up. This is a tryout for a sports activity, not a beauty contest, and you should look appropriate. A little foundation to cover any spots or even out skin tones, light blush, and a tonal eye shadow should be plenty. Leave the eyeliner and lipstick at home.
- No swearing! You are a positive role model, and swearing is a negative thing that will reflect badly on you. First of all, no one enjoys being around someone who swears. Secondly, it shows you cannot handle the task confidently.

At the tryout, be sure to listen closely to all the instructions given by the coaches and judges.

The most important thing that you can bring to your tryout is a *smile*. You will feel nervous inside, but try not to let it show. Now is not the time to be shy. Keep your head up and make eye contact with the coach and judges. When you give your name and say "hello," make sure you speak in a clear, loud, confident voice.

Remember, you don't have to *feel* confident to look it! Lots of people who seem to be completely self-assured on the outside are actually shaking inside. If you read interviews with many famous actors or singers, they describe feeling petrified before walking out on the stage each night. But once they are out in front of the audience, they become focused on their work and all their fears go away.

In fact, experts say that a little bit of nervousness is a good thing, because it helps to keep you focused. Many times, being overly confident can work against you, making you less focused and less "on," which can lead to mistakes or sloppiness.

The judges are not expecting you to do everything perfectly. What they are looking for is your potential for growth and your determination to not give up on yourself, even during a difficult move. If you do mess up on a cheer or chant during your tryout, just keep going and make up for it at the end with an extra loud cheer and increased energy. If you mess up on a stunt, the best tactic is to address the judges with confidence and say, "I know I can do better! May I try again?"

TIPS TO REMEMBER FOR PERFORMING THE JUMPS

- Keep your toes pointed when in the air.
- Keep your legs extended as much as possible and level with each other. Straight, even legs show technical mastery and will earn you more points than height alone.
- Keep your feet together for a clean landing.
- Keep good posture with your shoulders back, chest and chin up, and eyes looking at the judges.
- Keep your arm motions coordinated with the jumps in strong, sharp movements with straight arms that do not break at the wrist.
- Don't forget to smile and have fun.

TIPS TO REMEMBER FOR CHEERS AND CHANTS

- Use a loud voice to show you can lead a crowd.
- Keep good posture to help your voice be more powerful.
- Project your voice from your diaphragm, not your throat.
- Pace your cheer. Don't go too fast or you won't be understood; if you speak too slowly your words could be drawn out.
- Keep your pronunciation clear with full "S" and "T" sounds.
- Yell actual *words*, not "Yeah!" or "Woo." Try "Go team," "Let's go, Bears," etc.
- Use chants as you take the court and leave the court.

Did I Make the Squad?

At the tryout, you would have been assigned a number. Within a week or so of the tryouts, the coach will post the numbers of the girls who make the squad as well as those of the alternates.

If you find your number on the board, congratulations! You are now part of the squad and your first move as a school representative should be to thank the coaches and tell them that you look forward to a great season.

If your number is not listed, don't despair. Although it is disappointing, you should use the opportunity to show the coach what you are really made of. Seek out the coach and thank him or her for the opportunity. Say that you are still interested and would like to find out what areas need work so that you can address them for tryouts the following year.

Lucky Number 7

Christine Farina

My very first cheerleading tryout was when I was 13 years old and one of over a thousand students at St. Francis Prep School. That year, 170 girls tried out for the coveted 18 spots on the cheerleader squad.

I knew I had a lot of spirit, and deep inside I felt that I could do a good job and had what it takes. I really wanted to cheer more than anything. But I also knew that I was not the most talented or the most flexible girl trying out. I knew that if I was going to make the squad, I was going to have to work hard.

Every day I would stand in front of my mirror and practice my jumps. I'd ask myself, "Were my toes pointed, were my legs level, was my chin up, and were my movements clean?" Since my biggest challenge was flexibility, I stretched and stretched and stretched! I felt like I sat in a split for three days to make sure that I'd be able to have the highest toe touch at tryouts.

I will never forget my feelings of joy and achievement the day the numbers were posted and I saw my number 7 on the board! I think of it as my lucky number to this day. I remember running to all my teachers who had given me positive encouragement and recommendations, saying, "I made it! I made it!" Becoming a cheerleader changed my life. But even as a member of the team, I never took it for granted that I was part of the squad. I never stopped practicing in the mirror and continued to work on my flexibility by always stretching, stretching, stretching. And in my junior and senior years at college I won the Best Jumper Award!

Christine Farina and Matt Jones celebrate their third National Championship after the 2009 season.

My Life as an Alternate

Calison James, Hofstra Cheer Squad

I cheered in high school for three years, and my main reason for choosing Hofstra University was my admiration for its cheer team and my desire to be part of it. While I was thrilled when I received the e-mail that said I made the team for cheering at games, my coach had a private meeting with me to explain that I did not make the competition squad. It was really hard news for me to take, and at first I was very upset. My coach explained that it was important for the team to have the very best people on the mat and that my skills were just not there. I understood completely but was still disappointed. I have been an alternate for two years and have never had the opportunity to compete, but I have found ways to get over my disappointment and participate in a positive way.

Things I think about to turn my attitude around:

* ❇ I'm lucky to be physically fit.
* ❇ I tried my best.
* ❇ There is a reason for everything.
* ❇ Don't ever give up because anything is possible.
* ❇ The cheer team is like my family, and I want them to succeed.
* ❇ It's not all about me!

I like coming up with ways to be part of the competition squad even though I am not traveling with them. For example, before Nationals I'll make everyone a cute megaphone with quotes and pictures on it to hang above their bed in the hotel room. That way, they carry a little bit of me with them that I hope will help give them motivation and spirit.

My coach talks about how the team is a family and we should always think of others. This attitude has spread to other areas of my life. At home, when my sister does something great, instead of feeling jealous when my mom and dad praise her, I can genuinely feel happy and excited for her too. Although I continue to work on my cheer skills and hope that one day I will make the competition squad, I know that being an alternate has taught me a valuable life lesson that I feel lucky to have learned.

The first wealth
is health.
—Ralph Waldo
Emerson

STRETCHES, CONDITIONING DRILLS, AND EXERCISES

CHAPTER 7

DISCARD

STAYING PHYSICALLY FIT IS important for cheering and for life. Being in good physical condition will help you emotionally, because you'll find it easier to maintain an easy-going attitude by releasing endorphins (chemicals that make you feel better) every time you work out. You will still have

bad days and good ones, but fitness can help you feel more in control and less like you are on a rollercoaster of emotions. As a cheerleader, your school expects you to be at your best as often as you can. Feeling happy, calm, and in control helps you to achieve your personal best.

Being fit can help you focus better as well, because those same endorphins help to calm the mind and allow you to concentrate on the task at hand, keeping your mind from wandering. Obviously, you will be able to accomplish schoolwork and other tasks more efficiently and effectively when you apply more of your brainpower. When you are performing stunts or at a half-time show, you really need to have all of your focus in the moment.

In addition to the mental benefits of being in shape, there are the obvious physical benefits. The stretches and conditioning drills in this chapter are selected to increase your flexibility, balance, and muscle tone while training your body to make the quick, precise movements that are the mark of a skilled cheerleader. These exercises will also help you to increase your stamina so you'll have the energy to make the most of your practice time and will be able to stay energized for an entire game or competitive routine.

Before practice, prepare your muscles with a 10- to 15-minute warm-up. Muscles with good blood flow are more elastic and therefore less prone to injury. To get that increased blood flow, you need to raise your heartbeat with some cardio work, get your muscles moving, and get them stretched. It should feel good to get your body moving, so whether you are practicing alone at home or with your team, crank up your favorite music and have fun with it.

Warm-up Moves and Cardio

An effective, two-minute, full-body warm-up can be achieved by performing each of these moves for 20 seconds each. This warm-up will get your blood pumping and will literally warm up your body to prepare it for exercise.

RUNNING IN PLACE
Remain in one spot while you run in place and lift your knees up as high as you can. Pump your arms vigorously while you are running.

JUMPING JACKS
Start with your feet together and your arms at your sides. As you jump with your feet a little more than hip distance apart, raise your arms at your sides and clap them together over your head. Jump back to starting position while returning arms to sides, and repeat.

SLIDE LEFT/RIGHT
Start with feet together and arms at your sides, then slide your left foot out to the side and bend your left knee as if in a squat position. As you slide your

leg out, lift both your arms out to the sides at shoulder height. As you bring your left leg back in, also bring your arms back to starting position. Repeat to the right and continue for 20 seconds.

RUNNING IN PLACE gets your whole body awake and ready to move.

BASIC GRAPEVINE AND VARIATIONS
Start in standing position with feet together. With your right foot, take a step to the right while extending arms out to both sides at shoulder height.

Next, move your left foot so that it crosses behind the right while you cross your arms in front of you. Then take another step to the right with your right foot while you extend arms out to the sides again. Finally, step your left foot together with your right foot while you clap your hands together. Repeat the sequence to the left. Start with a few of the basics and move with the music. You can then add variations. With a pivot turn: As you take your initial step to the right, turn your body in a full pivot clockwise until you are facing front again and your left leg is crossed behind your right. With a kick: At the end, instead of clapping you can raise your heel behind you and touch it with the opposite hand.

KICK BACK

KICK BACK—this exercise helps to stretch your thighs as you warm up.

Stand with your hands on your buttocks, palms facing outward. Kick your feet back as if running and try to touch your right hand with your right foot and your left hand with your left foot at each kick.

HEAD ROLLS

Drop your head to the right as if you want to touch your ear to your shoulder, but be sure to keep your shoulder and neck muscles relaxed. Gently roll your head so that your chin is pointed at your chest, then upward until your left ear is above your left shoulder. Then lift your chin toward the ceiling, dropping your head back, and continue around until you have made a full rotation. Roll again in the reverse direction.

HEAD ROLLS
loosen up your neck.
Tension can lead to
strained muscles.

ARM ROLLS

Stand with your feet together and arms out to your sides at shoulder height. Rotate your arms by moving them in small circles to the front. Increase the size of each circle until you have completed eight circles. Then start small again as you circle your arms in the reverse direction and increase the circles until you reach eight rotations.

Stretches

After the cardio portion of the warm-up, take a few extra minutes to stretch. This will ensure that your muscles transition comfortably from ordinary activity to the workout. The short-term benefits are reduced muscle aches and pains. Stretching at the end of a workout as part of your cool-down has long-term benefits that include toning muscles to look long and lean, not bulky.

SIDE STRETCH

Stand with your legs slightly wider than shoulder width apart. Rest your left hand on your hip. Reach over your head with your right hand. Bend your body to the left as if you were pulling yourself by your right hand. The focus of the gentle pull should be up and over toward the far wall. Reach long. Your arm should be over your head at a 45-degree angle. Be sure to keep your chest square and your shoulders back. Hold for a split second at the height of your stretch, then return to the upright posture and repeat on the other side.

RUNNER'S FRONT STRETCH feels so good and gets your muscles ready to move.

RUNNER'S STRETCH

Stretch one leg straight out behind you and balance on your toes while bending the forward leg until your thigh is parallel to the floor. Bend your body forward to rest your hands on your bent knee or on the floor to the sides of your forward foot. Feel the stretch in the thigh muscle of the leg extended back. Hold for a count of 10 and then without shifting the placement of your feet, straighten both legs while lowering your back heel to the ground. Your hips move back while you keep your chest as close as you can to your forward thigh. Hold for 10 counts. Repeat to the opposite side.

You'll feel the RUNNER'S BACK STRETCH in your hamstrings and calves.

THIGH STRETCH

Start in a standing position with feet together. Keeping your body straight, reach back with your right hand and grasp your right foot behind your body. Gently pull the foot toward your buttocks and feel the stretch in your thigh. Hold for 10 seconds and repeat on the left side.

Keep an upright posture with level hips for an effective THIGH STRETCH.

TOE TOUCH

Stand with your feet together and arms at your sides. Start by stretching forward and bend down to touch your toes with your fingertips. Once down, pull your head in toward your knees and try to touch your head to your knees without bending your legs. Hold for a count of 10.

TOE TOUCH STEP ONE; stretching forward.

TOE TOUCH STEP TWO; full extension down.

ARM STRETCH

Stand with feet together and extend one arm in front of you at shoulder height. With your other hand, gently pull the extended arm just above the elbow across your body at shoulder height as you feel a stretch in your shoulder. Exhale as you stretch to receive the maximum benefit and hold for a few seconds. Repeat the stretch with your other arm.

Most of the ARM STRETCH is really felt in the shoulder.

BUTTERFLY STRETCH

Sit on the floor with the soles of your feet together and pulled in as close to your body as possible. Stretch your muscles by pushing your knees gently down toward the floor.

The BUTTERFLY STRETCH is a great inner thigh warm-up for splits and jumps.

OPEN-LEG STRETCH

Sit on the floor with legs extended as far out to the sides. You should feel a slight stretch in your inner thigh and be able to keep your legs flat on the ground comfortably, with your feet flexed and toes pointed toward the ceiling. Being sure to keep both buttocks cheeks on the floor, raise your left arm over your head and extend down over your right leg. Stretch your left hand toward your right foot while keeping your chest open; don't cave inward. Hold for a count of 10 seconds, then lift up while sweeping your arm up toward the ceiling for added support. Repeat to the left side.

Repeat the above exercise with one leg drawn in so that your foot is in close to your body. Repeat with other leg drawn in.

The OPEN-LEG STRETCH helps keep your legs toned and relaxed while conditioning your torso.

FORWARD STRETCH

Sit with your back straight and both legs extended in front of you, feet flexed so that your toes are pointed at the ceiling. Raise your arms above your head and bend forward at the waist to reach for your toes. Keep your back as straight as possible. You will get a better stretch by keeping a flat, straight back and not reaching your toes rather than arching your back. Once you are at maximum reach, hold for a count of 10. Remember to breathe while you are stretching.

The FORWARD STRETCH should be modified for your own flexibility; only go forward as far as you can maintain proper form.

Using your breath to help you extend during the ONE-LEG STRETCH will allow you to get a deeper stretch.

ONE-LEG STRETCH

Sit with your back straight and one leg extended in front of you with your foot flexed. Bend the other leg so that the sole of the foot is flat against your inner thigh and as close to your hips as you can comfortably get it. Breathe in as you raise your arms above your head, and exhale slowly as you bend forward at the waist to lower yourself down over your extended leg. Feel that you are reaching for your toes, and keep your back as flat as possible. Having a curved back will not get you the benefits of the stretch. Relax and hold the stretch for a few seconds, then return to the starting position. Switch your legs and repeat on the other side.

SIT WITH THIGH STRETCH

Sit with your knees bent, feet flat on the floor, and your hands behind you for support. Lower both knees to one side, and try to keep your knees together as you reach the ground. Rock your legs over to the other side, and repeat a few times to loosen up your thighs and lower back.

The SIT WITH THIGH STRETCH really loosens up the joints and feels great.

The CAT STRETCH is derived from yoga and when used with breathing is an wonderful torso warm-up.

CAT STRETCH

Start on your hands and knees with your back straight. Inhale as you round your back upward (visualize an angry cat arching its back). Let your head fall toward the floor. Exhale as you release your back and gently curve your belly toward the floor as you raise your face to the ceiling. Remember, this is a gentle curve to warm up your spine—do not force or over-stretch the spine. Slow movements are most effective for this stretch. Do six repetitions.

STANDING TWIST

Stand with your feet hip-distance apart. Hold your hands at chest height, elbows out. Twist your torso from left to right while keeping your hips centered to the front. Twist six times to each side.

Running

Taking a run a couple of times a week can help your cardio and increase your stamina. While running regimens will vary on personal preferences, a one-mile distance is a good general guideline. Running at the end of a practice session adds more cardio to your overall workout while providing a perfect opportunity to work on your mental preparation. If you are a competitive cheerleader, this run is a great time to put on your headphones and listen to your routine music. As you run to the beat of the song, mentally review all the moves of your routine. Visualize at which points in the music you are to hit your spot and make your moves. Visualization trains your brain and your body to have muscle memory of all the moves and will help you perform better. Most world-class athletes use visualization techniques to improve their performance, because if you can see it in your mind, it is easier to actually do it. If you don't have time for a mile, then run for two minutes, thirty seconds—the length of a competition routine.

Conditioning Exercises and Drills

Finish your practice session with about 20 minutes of conditioning exercises. These exercises focus on strengthening three major areas that are essential to cheerleading: The *abdominal muscles*, which are your core strength (torso strength); *leg muscles* for jumping, lifting, and catching; and *arm muscles* for stunts, catching, and lift support. You should try to get through each of these exercises three to five times, doing them in a rotation.

CORE/ABDOMINAL

SIT-UPS

The sit-up is one of the main exercises for core strength. Core strength is important for cheerleaders to maintain proper posture in poses and improves balance. Having a strong core can reduce injuries because the muscles form a protective armor around the ribs and internal organs. There are many variations on the sit-up, but the basic version is to lie on your back with your knees up and feet flat on the floor. Keep your hands behind your head. Keep your neck straight and do not pull on your neck or head; use your stomach muscles to get you up. Raise yourself all the way to a sitting position. As you release your body down to the floor, go slowly to prevent injury and maximize the exercise.

SIT-UPS are a workout classic; there are multiple variations of arm and leg positions and degrees of crunch.

CRUNCH SIT-UPS WITH PARTNER

When working out with a partner, sit facing each other with legs bent and link your ankles with your partner's ankles. Do sit-ups (as described above) simultaneously, meeting face to face in a sitting position. There are variations you can do with your arms, including keeping them behind your head with elbows out and relaxed, holding arms at your chest with your elbows pointed down, or, if you have a medicine ball, try passing the ball between you each time you come up.

SQUAT THRUSTS

Squat thrusts use mainly core strength but also incorporate your legs and upper body. They build endurance and stamina and also increase your heart rate.

Stand with your feet a little wider than shoulder-width apart and your arms at your sides. Squat down so that your hips are as low as possible without being lower than your knees. Keep your back straight, your chest out, and your shoulders back. As you squat, bend your arms at the elbows with your palms facing each other.

When you are in full squat, place your hands on the ground in front of you and simultaneously thrust your legs out into a push-up position. Do not let your back bend up or down. You should have a straight line from your head to your feet. The best way to ensure that you are maintaining posture is to keep your abdominal muscles tight. Jump your feet back to the starting position and stand up.

Performed solo or with a partner, LEG LIFTS really engage your core.

LEG LIFTS

The leg lift is a great core exercise that is even more effective when done with a partner. Lie on your back with your partner standing above your head, their feet by your shoulders, and grasp their ankles. Keep your back flat on the floor while you raise your legs straight up into the air. As your feet reach your partner's hands that are stretched out in front of him or her, have your partner push your legs back down toward the floor. Do 15 leg lifts before switching positions with your partner, and then repeat twice more.

LEGS

Your legs are your primary source of power on jumps. These exercises will help to build that power and help you build the excitement.

FORWARD LUNGES

Stand with your feet shoulder-width apart and your hands on your hips. Take a long, smooth step straight forward about double your shoulder width. Bend your back leg so that your knee moves toward the floor, stopping about an inch away from the floor and not touching it. You will be on the ball of your back foot. Check that your front knee is right over your front foot, not overextended over the toes; your shoulders should be back, your chest out, and your back straight. Recoil to the starting position by pushing up with your front foot. Repeat on the same leg for a full 10 repetitions for beginners, until you switch to your other leg.

FORWARD LUNGES can be a stationary by returning the front foot to start or moving by bringing the back foot forward with each lunge.

WALL SITS look easy, but you'll feel the burn doing this thigh-strengthening exercise.

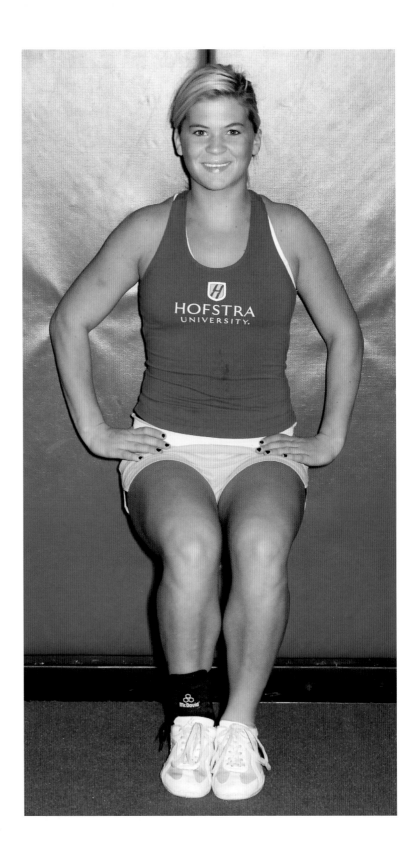

WALL SITS

The wall sit is a challenging exercise that will really strengthen your thigh muscles. Stand with your back against a wall and lower yourself down as if you were sitting in a chair, with your thighs at a 90-degree angle to your legs. Hold this position for one minute.

ARMS

PUSH-UPS

Start with your body face down on the floor. Place your hands flat on the floor at chest level, slightly wider than shoulder width but with elbows still close to your body. Your legs are close together, with your weight on the balls of your feet, or your knees if you need to modify the move. To protect your neck, look down and be sure to hold your head up so that your spine is in a straight line from your head all the way down your back. This straight line

PUSH-UPS are a tried and true exercise for strengthening that can be modified to be easier or harder.

includes keeping your butt level with the rest of your body; it should not be higher or lower. Use your arms to press your body up and down in a controlled motion. Do not allow your body to touch the floor during your down motion. Remember that quality is more important than quantity, so keep your form throughout.

HANDSTAND

The handstand is a gymnastics training exercise that increases your shoulder strength and flexibility. Stand facing a wall about 3 feet away. Place your hands on the floor a few inches away from the wall, and kick up into a handstand position with your feet touching the wall. Be sure that your arms are locked and your shoulders are shrugged so that they are next to your ears. Hold your body in this position for 20 to 30 seconds.

A gymnastic staple, the HANDSTAND strengthens the arms and shoulders while increasing balancing abilities.

Flexibility

While all cheerleaders need flexibility, the flyer position needs to work on different skills to be able to perform the arabesque, scorpion, scale, and heel stretch poses. To increase back flexibility, have your partner hold your leg and body in position for one-minute intervals. Practice the stretch three to five times within your conditioning rotation.

Working with a partner can help you stretch your muscles and increase your extensions.

The more advanced poses, like scorpion, are more easily perfected when assisted by a partner to ensure maximum stretch and proper positioning.

There is the enthusiasm of cheering on the sidelines, but stunting is what really wows the crowd.

CHAPTER 8

JUMPS, TUMBLING, AND STUNTS

EACH CHEERLEADER HAS HIS or her own reasons for participating, but a favorite part for many is the athletic portion—the opportunity to display gymnastic skills and stunting. Although a good squad makes it all look effortless, you can be assured that everyone starts with the basic moves and builds on them with crowd-pleasing variations and more highly skilled versions. In this chapter, we will look at some of the basic and intermediate skills in jumping, tumbling, and stunting that you will learn as a cheerleader. All jumps begin in start position with legs together and hands clasped in front of, and close to, your chest with elbows in tight to the body.

Much of the lift power in the TUCK is in the abdominal muscles.

Jumps

TUCK

Begin in start position. As you jump, raise your arms to a V position while your knees come up toward your chest with your legs together and feet pointed. Be sure to keep your chest up and facing forward; don't let it collapse toward your legs.

SPREAD EAGLE

From start position, raise your arms to a wide V position as you jump and spread your legs wide to the sides with your knees forward and toes pointed. You should resemble a giant X shape.

Daily practice of the basic jumps like the SPREAD EAGLE is a good routine to get into.

SIDE HURDLER

As you jump, extend one leg straight out to the side with your knee toward the ceiling and toe pointed. Your other leg is bent and level with your hip, knee facing forward. The arms are straight and in a T position matching the legs.

TOE TOUCH

From the start position, jump your legs into a spread-leg toe-touch position. Although the name of the jump suggests you will touch your toes, hit a nice T-motion at the height of the jump. Be sure to keep your chest and face up.

The **SIDE HURDLER** varies from the hurdler in the **T** shape arm position and the knee direction facing the ground.

In the **TOE TOUCH** your hands are fisted over the instep rather than actually touching the toes.

FRONT HURDLER

Turn at a 45-degree angle from the crowd. Split your legs front and back as you jump. Your front leg is bent at the knee facing the ground. Your back leg is extended, straight, and as high in front of you as possible. At the height of the jump, swing your arms to hit the touchdown motion (arms extended straight up with fisted hands).

The FRONT HURDLER is best viewed at a slight angle to the crowd to show off the split position.

PIKE is one of the more challenging jumps and is often performed sideways to the crowd to best display the air position.

PIKE

A pike is like doing a forward toe touch in the air. Jump with your legs out straight in front of you, legs together and straight. Reach down with your arms and hit candlesticks (arms straight and hands fisted near toes). Be sure to keep your face looking forward at the crowd.

DOUBLE 9

The double 9 gets its name from the shape you make with your arms and legs. One leg is straight in front and level with hip to form the back of a "9." The other leg is bent and level with the knee facing out to the side. At the height of the jump the foot on the bent leg touches the extended leg at the knee to form the loop. The arm position matches that of the legs while level with the shoulders: one arm extended in front while the other is bent, elbow out and hand touching the other elbow.

DOUBLE 9 is similar to the pike but with a bent arm and leg to form a 9 shape.

DOUBLE TOE TOUCH

The double toe touch is the basic toe touch done twice. When you land the first jump, your knees will be slightly bent. Use the momentum of that bend to power up into a second toe touch.

The first jump of the DOUBLE TOE TOUCH; the higher and wider the legs, the better.

Bent knees between the first and second jump will provide cushioning for the landing of the first jump and momentum for the second jump.

In the **DOUBLE TOE TOUCH, THE SECOND TOE TOUCH** should be as strong as the first.

A clean finish after a **DOUBLE TOE TOUCH** jump shows control of your balance.

Basic Tumbling Skills

FORWARD ROLL

Begin in a squat position balanced on the balls of your feet with your arms out in front. Lower your hands to the floor, and tuck your head to begin the roll. Be sure to roll onto your shoulders, not onto your neck. As you push off with your feet, keep your legs tucked as you roll over and back onto the balls of your feet. You can use your hands to push up or for balance as necessary.

For fun, try linking a few FORWARD ROLLS together to get across the mat.

CARTWHEEL

Begin by standing with your legs apart, one foot pointed in the direction you want to go, and your arms extended above your head. Look down at the ground where you will be placing your hands and then place your front hand (same hand as pointed foot) on the ground as you kick your legs over your head. Think of your body as a wheel that you are turning around by placing hand, hand then foot, foot. Like a wheel, your body should be flat when viewed from the side so your arms, torso, and legs are all aligned and directly over each other.

Keep your body perfectly flat for a CARTWHEEL that really resembles a wheel.

ROUND-OFF

The start of a round-off is similar to a cartwheel, except you will typically run into a round-off rather than beginning from a standing position. When in the upside-down vertical position, snap your legs together and land both feet at the same time with a bend in your knees and your arms extended. When you land, you should be facing the direction that you came from, not the front. The key to a good round-off is *speed*, so really push from your shoulders as you go through the motion to give yourself momentum.

BACK WALKOVER

A confident back bend is essential to a smooth BACK WALKOVER.

Before you attempt a back walkover, you should be comfortable with doing a basic backbend and have good strength in your arms and shoulders. Start by standing with legs hip-distance apart and arms over your head close to your ears. As you lean backward into your bend, instead of keeping both feet planted on the floor, lift one leg up into the air and use the momentum to carry you over so that your leading leg and then the following leg land on the floor behind your hands and you are able to stand up.

Advanced Tumbling Skills

These tumbling skills should not be attempted without expert supervision. They are listed here so that you know what they are and what you can strive for.

STANDING BACK HANDSPRING (BHS)

The standing back handspring takes the back walkover to the next level because you literally spring yourself backward. Begin by standing with your feet together. Your arms are at your sides and your back is straight. Your gaze should be straight in front of you with your chin level. Sit back as though you are about to sit in a chair. Just before you fall, swing your arms up forcefully and jump in a direction behind you (not straight up in the air). Your hands will touch the floor as your legs are in the air. Keep your eyes focused on the floor to keep from getting dizzy. Push off the floor and snap your legs together to land in a standing position.

A STANDING BACK HANDSPRING really takes your performance up an exciting notch.

Always try aerials like the STANDING BACK TUCK with proper supervision.

STANDING BACK TUCK

This move is similar to the back handspring in motion; however, your hands will not touch the ground as you flip backwards. Instead, when you reach the apex of your jump, tuck your legs in and grab your thighs with your hands briefly before un-tucking for the landing.

These basic and advanced gymnastic skills can be performed individually or combined in a routine for added impact. Some typical combinations include:

- Standing BHS/tuck, where you perform the BHS and then move right into the back tuck
- Round-off/BHS, where you keep the momentum from the round-off to push yourself right into the BHS
- Running round-off/BHS/back tuck

Stunts

Stunts involve two or more people that build levels by raising one person on top of the other(s). Stunts are real crowd-pleasers during games and pep rallies and are an essential part of competitive cheering. In this section, we'll review some of the basic stunts, of which there are many variations.

An all-girl stunt group typically has up to four bases and a flyer. A base is a cheerleader who stays on the ground and provides the primary support for the flyer. In addition to support, the bases also toss and catch and are the safety for the flyer. They must watch the flyer at all times to avoid mishaps. Bases are usually the strongest athletes on the team.

A pyramid is made when two or more stunt groups connect as the top girls connect arms, or when multiple levels are constructed with the flyers already in the air, acting as the primary base for another flyer. Most girls specialize in being either a base or a flyer, but good all-round cheerleaders are always versatile. It is recommended that you learn both jobs to ensure maximum communication as well as versatility. Regardless of body type and personal preference, there is a place for everyone in cheerleading.

When performing one-legged stunts, the main base will support the majority of the flyer's weight and will lift the toe and heel of the foot to increase forward/backward stability. The secondary base assists in lifting the flyer up and places one hand under the shoe and the other around the main base's wrist to give support.

The back spotter stands behind the stunt to help dip or jump the flyer into the side bases' hands. The back spotter also supports the flyer by holding onto her calves or ankles when in position or by giving additional support to the bases' wrists. If the flyer should fall backward, it's the back spotter's responsibility to catch her in order to avoid serious injury to the head, neck, and shoulders.

The flyer is the main focus of the stunt, and a good flyer will be a performer with a lot of personality that will project out to the crowd. Flyers are typically the members of the team that display excellent body control and positioning whether they are small in frame or have an athletic build. Flexibility is a definite plus, as it makes a flyer's performance more dramatic, but a strong core and excellent balance are essential. The key to a controlled performance is the ability to control one's weight by squeezing the muscles in the thighs, core, and shoulders and staying tight.

Some teams may also work with a front spotter, whose main responsibility is to prevent the flyer from falling forward but who also provides extra support and power in extended stunts. Another general spotter may stand behind, in front, or beside the stunt and stay attentive to the stunt at all times with arms raised, ready to assist.

Basic Stunts

Now that we have reviewed the different positions, let's look at the performance of some of the most common stunts.

THIGH STAND

In the thigh stand, two bases face each other in either a kneeling or standing-with-one-knee-bent position, with the sides of the bases' shoes touching. The back spotter holds the flyer at the waist and assists her in a dip and jump onto the bases' thighs. The flyer puts a hand on each base's shoulder for support and places one foot on a base's thigh to begin the mount. Once fully supported on the thighs, the bases wrap an arm around the flyer's legs with the other arm cradling her foot for additional support as the flyer reaches up with her arms for the hit position.

PREP

In the prep, the flyer stands with her feet at shoulder level of the bases. To begin, the bases face each other about a foot apart. The flyer is assisted up into the hands of the bases by the back spotter, jumping both feet into the bases' hands at about waist height. Once the flyer is in position, the back spotter supports her ankles or calves. Once the flyer is in the bases' hands, they raise her up so that her feet are even at their shoulder level. The flyer controls the stunt by the distance she keeps her legs apart and by moving the bases together or apart. The flyer/top girl hits the stunt when her legs are straight and tight and her arms hit a motion.

EXTENSION

The extension is similar to the prep with the difference in how high the flyer is lifted. Instead of the flyer's feet being supported at the bases' shoulder level, the bases lift until their arms are fully extended. The back spotter can hold either the flyer's ankles or support the bases' wrists, whichever they are tall enough to reach.

The PREP and EXTENSION are safe, easy stunts that are especially effective when used with a sign.

FULL DOWN, OR TWIST DOWN

An exciting option to the cradle dismount from both prep and extension, the full down dismount requires the bases to push the flyer into the air so that the flyer, keeping her body very tight and in a straight line, can rotate once before dropping into the cradle.

Once you've got the extension down pat, the QUARTER-UP EXTENSION is a fun variation.

QUARTER-UP EXTENSION

The mount is the difference in the quarter-up extension, a variation of the extension. The bases face each other with the flyer in the middle, facing one of the bases. The flyer puts one foot into the facing base's hands about waist height while the base at her back supports her at the waist. As the flyer is lifted into the extension position, she makes a quarter turn from facing the side to facing forward. The hit position is the same as in the original extension, with the nonsupporting leg fully extended and grasped by the corresponding hand.

STAIR STEP TO EXTENSION

The stair step to extension is a variation on getting into the extension and is similar to walking up stairs. With the bases in extension position, the flyer jumps into their hands at waist height. The flyer then takes the first step up by raising one foot to shoulder level of one base; in the next step she raises her other foot to the full extension supported by the other base; in the final step she raises her foot from the prep level to full extension. The full extension hit position is then taken with arms in a V form. The stair step variation can also lead into one-legged stunts.

STAIR STEP TO EXTENSION is an all-time cheer camp favorite.

GROUND-UP LIBERTY, OR LIB

To begin the ground-up liberty, the bases face each other while the flyer puts one foot into their cradled hands about waist height and the back base assists the flyer by holding her at the waist. The flyer, holding onto the bases' shoulders for support, pushes off the ground with the other leg and is lifted into the air with bases' arms extended and the back base supporting the ankle as well. Once balanced on one leg, the flyer bends the other knee and places her foot against the standing leg knee and extends her arms up into a V shape for the hit.

WALK-IN HEEL STRETCH

The walk-in heel stretch is a variation of the ground-up liberty. The difference is that the hit point has the nonstanding leg extended. As the flyer is raised into position, she simultaneously lifts her leg forward and up and grasps the extended leg with her hand in one smooth motion.

Once you've mastered the GROUND-UP LIBERTY, you are on your way to a whole lot more.

The WALK-IN HEEL STRETCH is an elite stunt that shows off a flyer's flexibility.

The ARABESQUE is a real crowd-pleaser with a big wow factor.

ARABESQUE

The arabesque is a variation of the lib with three bases working together to lift and support the flyer from the side position that is described in the quarter-up extension. Once the flyer is in the air, she points her nonsupporting leg straight out behind and her arms are stretched in a T position for the hit.

The **SCORPION** always impresses because it really shows off a flyer's flexibility.

SCORPION

Named for its resemblance to a scorpion's tail, this lib variation requires a lot of flexibility. The lift itself is from the side so that the bases are rotated in a way that one base has her back to the crowd and the back base is on the side. Once the flyer is in full extension, she grabs the foot of her nonsupporting leg from the back with both hands so that the toes are close to or touching the back of her head.

The **SCALE** is another crowd-pleaser that requires a lot of flexibility and skill that not many can achieve.

SCALE, OR SKATER

The scale, or skater, is a third lib variation where the bases are rotated. Once the flyer is in position in the air, she raises the nonsupporting leg up as if in a vertical split supported by her corresponding hand. Both arms are raised in the V formation for the hit position.

The key to a great
FULL UP is timing,
timing, timing.

FULL UP

The full up/360 variation for getting into a lib begins with the extension
formation for the bases. The flyer jumps into the bases' hands at waist
height and, with a rigid body and arms at her sides, pivots one full turn
around as the bases lift her into full extension. Once up, the flyer can hit the
liberty pose.

Practice Makes Perfect

All those perfect stunts and routines don't just happen by themselves. They require a lot of hard work and practice. What separates "the best" from "the rest" is the ability to keep working and practicing regardless of whatever else is going on. Whether you have a lot of schoolwork or just feel tired, know that when you enter practice, the rest of the world goes away for that time and you focus your energy and attention on cheer. Don't think about the pain or frustration of the moment, and remember to visualize what you want to achieve.

Pain is temporary; pride lasts forever.

Thomas Edison said "Genius is 1% inspiration and 99% perspiration." Practice hard so when it is your turn to shine, the crowd never sees you sweat.

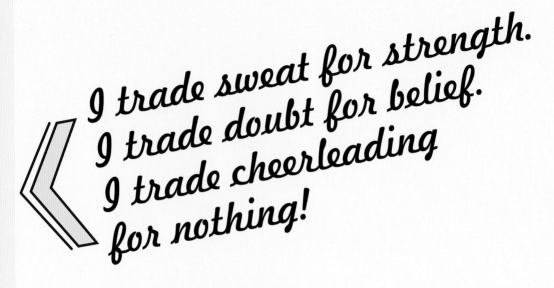

I trade sweat for strength.
I trade doubt for belief.
I trade cheerleading
for nothing!

CHEERS, CHANTS, AND MOTIVATION

A CHEERLEADER'S MAIN PURPOSE is to motivate and pump up the crowd and to encourage audience participation. Of course, cheerleaders should also motivate the athletes to perform at their best, and nothing beats hearing a stadium full of people chanting their team's name to keep them going. At the end of the day, games are more exciting and memorable for everyone, players and crowds alike, when the crowd is into it. Cheerleaders are on the front lines, getting the action started and keeping the enthusiasm going. Their motivational tools are the cheers and chants—and let's not forget the beloved mascots.

Practice makes perfect in cheerleading. In addition to practicing routines and individual skills, it is also important to memorize chants and cheers and to practice them in a loud, clear voice with lots of energy. A perfect cheerleading cheer should be catchy and simple and should always be performed energetically.

Finding Your Cheer Voice

Shutterstock

There are a number of ways to practice getting your voice to project across a gymnasium or field. First, learn to cheer from your diaphragm so that you do not wear out your throat. If you yell from your throat, you will be hoarse halfway through the game; you may even be without a voice the next day while your vocal cords heal! Your diaphragm is a sheet of muscle that extends along the bottom of your rib cage. This muscle separates your heart, lungs, and ribs (known as the thoracic cavity) from your abdominal cavity, and aids in respiration by expanding and contracting to draw in and expel the breath. Your diaphragm lends strength and power to your breath so you will be able to cheer for extended periods without losing your voice. Singers use their diaphragms to control their voices over their entire range with strength and longevity without damage to their vocal cords. To identify how to use your breath properly when you cheer, lie down on your back with your legs relaxed and out straight, put your hands on your upper stomach, and take a deep breath in. You should feel your stomach *expand* and get larger. Many people have a tendency to breathe backward and suck their stomach *in* when they breathe in. If you think about it, your lungs are like a balloon that is filling with air and should expand as you breathe in. You can also breathe into your stomach, take a deep breath, and expand just your stomach. On the next inhale, try filling your stomach first and then your lungs. Exhale slowly, emptying your stomach first and then your lungs, so that it feels like a wave of air through your torso—this is the correct way to breathe.

Take a deep breath in, open your mouth, and make an "Ahhhh" sound as you exhale. You should feel the strength in your voice coming from your diaphragm, not your throat. Your throat should feel relaxed, simply vibrating as the flow of air passes through. When speaking or cheering while using your breath correctly, you may find that your voice sounds deeper than you are used to. This is perfectly normal and can make you sound more self-confident, a great benefit when speaking (or cheering) in front of a group.

To practice using your cheer voice, try lying on your stomach while belting out cheers. You will feel the air expand into your stomach and lungs with each breath in. As you release the air for the subsequent contraction, feel the sound resonate up and through your throat. Keep your throat open in the back and *relaxed* to get the best sound without stress or tension.

Practice your cheer voice with a partner as well. Stand on opposite sides of a field, and practice a cheer using your diaphragm to project the sound. Your partner should be able to hear every word clearly, and you should feel a powerful, strong voice with no strain on your throat or vocal cords.

Picking Your Cheer and Chants

Cheers have come a long way from the famous:

> We've got spirit, yeah, yeah,
> We've got spirit, yeah, yeah,
> We've got what,
> What,
> What,
> What,
> What, what, what, what, what,
> We've got spirit!!

While there are a number of classic cheers for you and your squad to choose from, you may want to try making up some of your own. Whether you are selecting a classic or inventing a new one, there are some basic guidelines for getting the most out of your cheers.

The two most important parts of a cheer or chant are *words* and *rhythm*. If you combine these effectively, you might even create an earworm—something that gets in your head and won't go away. People could be walking around with your cheer in their heads for days! Without a good combination of words and rhythm, the crowd may be confused and unable to join the fun.

WORDS

Look for *short words* of one or two syllables each. These are easy to learn, say, and repeat.

Look for *hard words*—words that have hard consonants and vowel sounds. For example, "Go" and "Beat" are hard, short words. "Their," "Them," and "Let's" are softer words that have less impact.

When you combine words for a cheer, aim for a high number of short, hard words in the phrase. "Go, Fight, Win!" is composed of all short words with the first and last being hard, so there are more hard words than soft. "Let's beat them!" is not as effective because the first and third words are both soft.

Grin and Bear It
A good cheerleader needs to keep smiling even if the team is losing to its biggest rival. No matter how hard a stunt or a cheer is, you have to keep that grin intact!

TIP:

Belt It Out

You have to have pipes if you're to be a great cheerleader. Let's hear it now in a loud, clear voice!

RHYTHM

Think simple, basic rhythms with only three or four beats. You can divide up some of the beats to incorporate longer words, such as the name of your team or town, but remember: The simpler the better. Often, the best way to get the crowd involved is by chanting one word and one beat repeatedly, such as "Fight! Fight! Fight!"

The words don't have to pull all the weight when it comes to rhythm. Clap your hands, stomp your feet, or even get your pep band to join in with some percussion; just be careful not to drown out the words in all the excitement! Keeping your chants and cheers in short, hard words will help make sure they're always heard.

There some sample cheers to get you started at the end of this chapter.

MOTIONS

The final touch to a great cheer is the presentation to the crowd. Pairing up the words and beats to frequent arm movements can really sell it. Remember to keep your body taut with good posture and no extra movements to detract from the impact of the main motion. Your movements should be sharp, clean, and snappy for both a better-looking group performance and better viewing from the distance of the stands.

HAND POSITIONS

There are three basic hand positions: clap, blades, and sparkles. It may seem silly to give instructions on how to clap your hands, but it's very important that your teammates are all on the same page. If your squad lines up to clap with different arm, hand, and elbow positions, you will look messy and unprepared. Follow these simple guidelines to ensure a crisp, unified-looking squad.

The basic clap uses slightly cupped hands to maximize sound. Clasp your hands just under your chin, angled slightly away from your body. As you clap, keep your elbows close to your sides.

Blades position is similar to basic clap, but your hands are held palms together with fingers pointing upward like a blade. Your thumbs should be held tightly against your fingers with no space between.

Hand sparkles are when you hold your hands taut, with outstretched fingers spread wide apart and palms facing the crowd while you make a shimmy motion with your wrists. The positioning of the sparkles will change based on your routine.

iStockPhoto

Come on Get Snappy
A good cheerleader's moves are always tight and sharp. When you clap, your arms should be in front of your face. Have a buddy put her hands on your shoulders and learn to clap in the space between.

TIP:

ARM POSITIONS

There are several standard arm positions that will help you build an effective cheer or chant routine. Your hands should be in a fist or blades, and your arms should be tight. Your basic starting position, called clean, is standing at attention with your arms at your sides.

Beginning with the alphabet positions, these poses are strong silhouettes for distance viewing as well as being useful to literally spell things out on the field, such as "Victory" and "Team."

Give me a "V"!

A high V is made by extending your arms up and slightly out to form a V. You should be able to see your wrists with your peripheral vision.

The broken high V is made by bending your elbows from the high V position so that your forearms fold over your upper arms and your hands face downward next to your shoulders.

A low V is actually an upside-down V with your arms down and to the side and slightly in front of you.

Give me a "T"!

To make the T, extend your arms straight out to the sides and parallel to the ground.

For the broken T, from the T position bend your elbows so that your forearms fold over your upper arm and your hands rest at shoulder height.

VERTICAL MOTIONS
Touchdown

In the touchdown, your arms are extended above your head, parallel and close to your head. Your knuckles should face each other.

A low touchdown is with arms extended down to the ground in front of your body and parallel to each other; your hands are fisted with palms facing and thumbs toward crowd.

Table Top

To make a table top, bend your arms up so that your wrists are near your shoulders. Be sure to keep your elbows tucked in to your sides.

High Punch

Also called number one, the high punch is made is with one arm extended upward and close to your ear with your knuckles facing over your head (not facing the crowd). Your other arm is bent with your fisted hand on your hip.

DIAGONAL MOTIONS

Diagonals

Make a diagonal line across your body with your arms by stretching one arm up and the other arm down in the opposite direction.

Checkmark

To form a checkmark, your right arm is extended diagonally up and your left arm is in the position for table top, where your arm is bent and your hand is in front of your shoulder with the elbow tucked in to your side.

Sample Cheers and Chants

When creating a cheer or chant, use basic information like your team name, mascot name, school colors, or the name/initials of your school. Of course, using your opponent's team name or mascot name has its place too!

The (x) in these cheers designates a clap. Use short, hard words around the team name, which can also be alternated:

Go (x) Cubs (x) Go (x-x-x-x)
Fight (x) Cubs (x) Fight (x-x-x-x)
Win (x) Cubs (x) Win (x-x-x-x)

These are some real classics!

Lean to the Left

Lean to the left,
Lean to the right,
Stand up, sit down,
Fight! (x), Fight! (x), Fight! (x)

Stand Up and Clap Your Hands

Hey, all you Mustang fans,
Stand up and clap your hands!
Go Mustangs go (x), go Mustangs go!
Hey, all you Mustang fans,
Stand up and wave your hands!
Go Mustangs go (x), go Mustangs go!

1, 2, 3, 4

1, 2, 3, 4, come on (x), come on (x), yell go Bears go!
Go! (x) Bears! (x) Go! (x)
1, 2, 3, 4, come on (x), come on (x), yell beat those Cougars!
Beat! (x) Those! (x) Cougars! (x)
Go! (x) Bears! (x) Go! (x) Beat! (x) Those! (x) Cougars! (x)

Hey, Fans

Hey (x) fans! (x) In the stands! (x)
Give our team (x) a helping hand! (x)

Extra! Extra!

Extra! Extra!
Read all about it!
The Cougars are here,
And we're proud to shout it!
Here we go, Cougars,
Here we go! (x-x)

Keep It Up

Keep it up (x), keep it up (x),
Keep that Cougar spirit up!
Keep! (x) It! (x) Up! (x-x) Yeah! (x)

(Team Name) Beat

Now you've got that Tiger beat,
Let me hear you stomp your feet!

Clap/Stomp

Clap your hands! (x-x-x)
Stomp your feet! (s-s-s)
Clap your hands! (x-x-x)
Stomp your feet! (s-s-s)
We're the Hawks that can't be beat!

iStockPhoto

Learn the Lingo

In any sport, there are terms and moves. If you learn cheer lingo before tryouts, you'll impress the coach and learning will go more smoothly for you.

Good Luck Charms and Motivational Rituals

It's been said that good luck comes to those who work for it. Cheerleaders certainly work for their luck by putting in lots of practice time. But that doesn't mean we don't try to squeeze a little extra luck out at the last minute!

At the Murphy School, the cheerleaders sit cross-legged in a circle and hold on to each other's feet. They all chant, "I'm proud to be a Murphy cheerleader because . . ." and then take turns finishing the sentence with whatever they are feeling that day like "you all feel like sisters to me" or "it's so much fun!"

They also sing songs to get the nerves out and pump themselves up. One of their favorites is "Little Sally Walker," where they stand in a big circle.

Little Sally Walker,

Walking down the street,

She had nowhere to go,

So she stopped in front of me and said,

"Hey girl, do your thing, do your thing! Don't Stop."

At the last line, one girl does a dance move that all the others then mimic. They then sing again and repeat until all the girls have had a chance to "do their thing."

At another school, The Oceanside varsity cheer squad loves getting new T-shirts made up for each season to motivate them. It all started as a joke when their coach was trying to open a jar with a tight lid and said to herself, "Man, strength and anger—that's what I need to feel like to get this jar open!" When the coach shared her way of pumping herself up, everyone laughed and thought it would make a great motivational saying that would be their special thing. So they had T-shirts made up with the phrase "Man, Strength and Anger." For basketball season, they have "Lib It Up" on their shirts to remind them to have fun while using a pun on the liberty pose.

Here some cheerleaders share their personal good luck charms or rituals that they do as a squad.

> "Last year I wore the same sports bra for every competition. It felt right and gave me confidence. I may have to find a new one for this year!"
>
> - Francesca, age 15

Marissa, age 16

I'm a very superstitious person and a very religious person. It may seem silly, but there is a thing that I do before I'm about to do a new stunt, or cheer at a game, or anything that takes a lot of courage. I cross my fingers, I knock on wood, I do the sign of the cross, because I am very religious and I go to church with my family, and I clap and I smile as if I were cheering for a crowd. I'll usually do it quietly to myself, but my bases have seen it a million times. And when I do it all at once, I feel I've almost wiped out all the bad luck and all the things that could go wrong and am now prepared do whatever I'm about to do. And even when I'm getting down about what I'm doing, it gives me that extra push and extra smile, and gives me the understanding and purpose of what I'm doing and why I'm there.

Marissa demonstrates the "good luck routine" she created to help prepare herself for challenging stunts and competitions.

"I actually have a lot of superstitions. Before a competition I'll wear the same bobby pins in my hair, or I have to put my makeup on the same way, or I have to use the same applicator for my makeup. When I get into the arena, I have to walk a certain way—really crazy stuff like that. I have a lot of rituals, and they calm me down when I am a little anxious."

- Gabrielle, age 16

"Our team has a [good luck] ritual. We always tend to pray and say positive things before we go on and compete, or before games we do special cheers and chants and get pumped and ready to go."

- Ivette, age 17

Team Mascots

Mascots are an exciting and entertaining way to spread team spirit and get fans more involved in the game. A playful confrontation with the opposing team's mascot or fans can cause quite a stir!

Shutterstock

Shutterstock

Shutterstock

Look your best to be your best

BEAUTY, HAIR, AND MAKEUP

CHAPTER 10

Grooming and Personal Care

WHETHER YOU CHEER FOR your school, gym, or both, your preparation for cheer time should start with a healthy regimen of proper eating and plenty of sleep so that you can perform at your best. We cover nutrition and tips for eating properly and getting a good night's sleep in Chapter 11. If you establish good eating and sleeping habits now, they will last you for a lifetime.

Grooming is part of good representation and shows that you care. Even more importantly, it can be a reflection of your inner desire for happiness and the ability to achieve your goals. Dress for the part you want to play in life.

Shutterstock

DRESS

Grooming includes being neatly dressed on a daily basis. Your clothes should be age- and school-appropriate and not overly revealing. How you dress can say a lot about you. As a school representative, project the image of someone who has respect for herself. Presenting yourself in a neat and clean manner will show that you are a capable, well-rounded individual.

HAIR

Whether at practice, on game days, or at competition, your hair should be pulled back off your face. It should not be down or even half up. It doesn't look good to have your hair flying in your face and it can be hazardous during routines. Pulling your hair back will also protect your skin from breakouts, because sweaty hair on your face can cause pimples. You may want to show extra school spirit by tying your ponytail with a ribbon or bow in your school colors. If your hair is too short for a ponytail, you can pin a ribbon in it, but be sure to pin it off your face.

MAKEUP

Your makeup should be light enough that it doesn't run or get clumpy if you get warm and sweat. Cheering at events is an athletic activity, so you shouldn't look like a runway model with heavy makeup. You should wear only enough makeup to give you some stage presence and make you stand out from a distance. Before practice, it's best to clean off all makeup to avoid breakouts.

NAILS

Keep your nails trimmed short. Long nails can be a safety hazard when cheering—they can get snagged and caught on clothes or hair, or accidentally scratch your teammates. Clear polish is the best look for cheering because colored polishes can be distracting and take away from the overall sharpness of a routine.

JEWELRY

Do not wear jewelry when cheering or practicing. Not only is it distracting, it can be a hazard if it gets caught on clothing or pulled.

ATTIRE

During practice you should wear a tight-fitting top (such as a tank top), cotton shorts with no pockets, and girls should wear sports bras. Baggy shirts and pockets can be safety hazards as others' hands and shoes can get caught in them. A pair of cheerleading shoes with a rubber sole should also be worn.

During games or competition your uniform should be neatly pressed and clean with no stains. Your shoes should be brushed and clean. It is *your responsibility* to be sure that your uniform is washed and neat, and this sets a good impression for the entire squad.

Finding the right attire and makeup for your squad is all part of the fun. The possibilities are almost endless, so get creative and have fun! *Courtesy Razzle Dazzle Cosmetics*

What you will need:

* Mineral foundation pressed powder (should match your skin tone)
* Shimmer powder (silvery)
* Eyeliner powder or pencil (blue or school color)
* Blush
* Mascara wand
* Lip gloss (clear or sheer pink)
* Large blush/powder brush
* Angled liner brush
* Placement eye shadow brush

Professional Makeup Artist/ Hairstylist Tips

You will need different makeup and hairstyling for high school versus All-Star cheering. Stephanie Lombardi of Razzle Dazzle Cosmetics shares tips and techniques for both.

HIGH SCHOOL MAKEUP

High school makeup requires a light, natural look that will give your face enough pop to be seen from the bleachers.

STEP ONE

Apply a mineral foundation pressed powder. You can use either a compact or loose powder and apply with a large blush brush. Tap the powder all around the face for a light, even finish and to eliminate shine from sweating or oily skin. Powder will also cover any slight imperfections. A pure mineral foundation is all natural with no harsh chemicals to keep your young skin looking young.

STEP TWO

Use a placement eye shadow brush to apply a coat of light shimmer over the entire eyelid. Apply heavily below the eyelid crease and lightly above the crease up to the brow line.

The overall effect of shading with blush should be very subtle but will help to give your face definition from a distance.

The application of a silvery shadow will allow you to keep a natural look while giving the eyes more pop and expression.

If your school colors complement your face, eyeliner is a great place to incorporate them in a subtle but effective way.

STEP THREE

An eyeliner pencil may be used, but powder with a thin angled brush will give you more control. Your angled brush can be wet slightly to give extra control when applying as eyeliner. Beginning on the eyelid, start from the inside of the eye and work toward the outer edge by tapping the powder gently along the top of the eyelashes. For a natural look, stop the liner at the edge of the eyelid and do not extend past the lid.

Beneath the eye, use an angled brush with silver powder and tap along underneath the lower lashes to make your eyes stand out.

If you find that you have any shimmer dust where it shouldn't be, use a makeup wipe or large brush to gently clean your face.

STEP FOUR

Using a waterproof mascara, remove the wand and wipe any excess residue on the tip of the wand on a tissue before applying to avoid clumping.

Begin with the bottom lashes and apply underneath the lashes in a motion that wraps the lashes around the wand. By applying from the bottom, you are plumping the lashes as you coat them. Use the tip of the mascara wand to coat any hard-to-get areas. Apply to both lower lashes before moving on to the upper lashes to allow the lower lashes to dry and avoid smudging your mascara.

For the upper lashes, apply the mascara first to the top and finish by applying to the bottom of the lashes so that you are brushing them up as your final touch. This technique will allow the mascara to really make your eyes pop.

If you find mascara on your face, use the large brush or makeup pad to gently clean your face.

STEP FIVE

If your natural lip color is very close to your skin color, you may need to give your lips a little more pop by using a sheer pink gloss. If the gloss smudges while applying, use a cotton swap or makeup sponge to clean your lip line.

To bring out your lips, apply a clear gloss for a natural yet polished appearance.

STEP SIX

Apply a finishing layer using a large brush and pressed powder. Put a light amount of blush onto a large brush, and tap the bristles on a tissue to get rid of excess. Brush the blush over the top of the cheekbone to add a rosy glow. Lightly brush onto the tip of your chin, tip of your nose, and the top of forehead near your hairline.

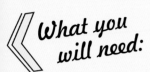

What you will need:

* Rattail comb
* Brush
* Clear rubber band
* Hairspray
* Shine spray

HIGH SCHOOL HAIR

The most important elements of hairstyling for high school cheering events are neatness of appearance and keeping it off your face. A good position for a ponytail is the center of the crown (not on the top of the head, but a little further back than a high ponytail). Here are the steps to making a great ponytail that will hold up during all of your cheering activities:

STEP ONE

Start at the front of your head just above your forehead, and gather a section of hair. Using a rattail comb and starting about 5 inches up from the root, push down the hair so that it bunches up; this is called teasing or backcombing. You can tease fairly large sections at a time since you will not be keeping the tease fully in, only using it to add extra body. Once you have teased a section, spray that section with a little hairspray for hold and let it fall to the side while you work on the next section, moving from front to back. With each section, comb out any knots and then go a few inches up from root and backcomb down and spray. Repeat only until you get to the crown area; you do not need to do your whole head.

Teasing the hair a little bit will keep your style from looking too harsh and tight.

Add shine spray all over before you brush, as this will not only add sheen to your hair but will make it more manageable and a little slicker.

Most bows come on a band that is affixed in the same manner as the rubber band.

STEP TWO

Use a brush to smooth your hair back so that the top is sleek. The tease will still be in a little bit to give softness to the look. When smooth, use both hands to gather hair at the center of the crown where you want the ponytail. Use a brush to smooth the top and the hair once more.

STEP THREE

Fasten using a clear rubber band. The thicker the rubber band, the more support you'll have. If your squad uses a hair accessory, add it now. Once your accessories are in place, flare the ponytail out a little for more volume, and spray again liberally with hairspray to keep your hair in place and out of your face. Finish with an overall application of shine spray to give your hair a professional look.

ALL-STAR MAKEUP

All-Star makeup can be dramatic and fun with lots of sparkle and pizzazz in colors that coordinate with your uniform.

STEP ONE

Apply a mineral foundation pressed powder. You can use either the compact or loose powder and apply with a large blush brush. Tap the powder all around your face for a light, even finish. This powder will eliminate shine from sweating or oily skin and will cover any slight imperfections. A pure mineral foundation is all natural with no harsh chemicals to keep your young skin looking young.

STEP TWO

With a placement eye shadow brush, lightly apply a silvery shimmer dust to the entire lid as a base that illuminates the eye.

TIP:

Silver shimmer helps to create an eye-popping look.

What you will need:

* Mineral foundation pressed powder (should match your skin tone)
* Shimmer powder (silvery)
* Eyeliner powder or pencil (blue or school color)
* Blush
* Mascara wand
* Lip gel (pink or red)
* Lip glitter
* Large blush/powder brush
* Angled liner brush
* Placement eye shadow brush
* Stick-on stars

There are many different ways to create an exciting eye using cream shadows that coordinate with your team colors. You can make "wings" like Cleopatra, a symbol for your team, or simply apply the team colors boldly defined. I like using cream shadow because it's easy to correct. If you are creating wings or shapes that should match on each eye, you can match them more easily and with less mess than a powder. It takes some practice to get your eyes even, so you'll want to try this a few times before your first performance. **Courtesy Razzle Dazzle Cosmetics**

Apply liner slowly and carefully to avoid mess, and use a very thin stream.

STEP THREE

Use a placement eye shadow brush to apply shadow softly to the lid in the desired shape. Highlight with silver or liner.

If you are making wings, cover the entire lid below your eye crease and extend in wings at the outer edges. End the wings at a point even with the end of your eyebrow line.

Follow along the top of the wing with silver. Silver cream shadow really makes the eyes bright and pops the color for great facials.

Add a few drops of white cream shadow to the inside area of the eye below the brow line and above the color. Gently smudge with your finger along the base of the brow on the top and following the color line underneath.

STEP FOUR

Apply liquid eyeliner for a clean look. Go slowly. Follow the lash line of your upper lid with a thin stream of liner. Go very lightly or else your eye will look too dark. Start from the outer edge of the lid and work your way in toward the bridge of your nose.

Cream shadow needs time to dry, so do one eye at a time and leave the eye closed for a few seconds to allow drying. Cream eye shadows will dry at different rates depending on the amount of oil in your skin, so give your shadow time to dry for a lasting, nonsmudge look.

Highlighting the edges of the color shadow with silver illuminates the eye. *Courtesy Razzle Dazzle Cosmetics*

STEP FIVE

Apply waterproof mascara to avoid raccoon eyes. Starting with the lower lashes, look up at the ceiling, pull the skin under your eye down slightly with one hand while using the other to gently coat your lashes from underneath for the best volume. For the top lashes, coat the upper part of the lashes first and finish with upward curling motions to open the eyes. If necessary, gently clean up any stray mascara flakes using a cotton ball, cotton swab, or makeup sponge.

STEP SIX

Dip a large brush into some powder blush and tap off the excess. Lightly brush upward from the apples of your cheeks to your hairline, just above the ear. Softly dab a little blush on your chin, the tip of your nose, and your hairline around the forehead to give definition to the face. If you have a high hairline, putting some blush along it can bring more focus to your face and minimize your forehead.

Glitter applied on top of lipstick can help create a sparkling smile. Check out the catalogs of companies that specialize in cheerleading cosmetics for great ideas and exciting new combinations. *Courtesy Razzle Dazzle Cosmetics*

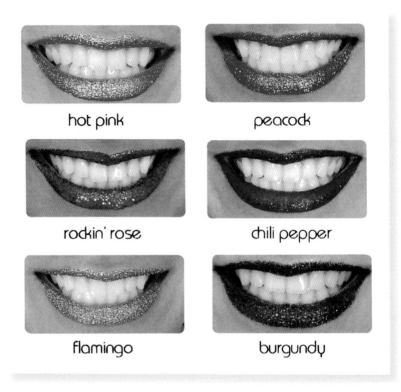

hot pink

peacock

rockin' rose

chili pepper

flamingo

burgundy

STEP SEVEN

Star stickers are a quick and fun way to add extra sparkle to your performance. You'll need to apply them to clean, dry skin that has no moisturizer or foundation, so wipe the area that you wish to apply the stickers to with a cotton ball. Simply peel the stickers off the backing and stick them where you wish. Use a mirror to be sure they're evenly placed, especially if you use stars by each eye.

STEP EIGHT

Apply lip gloss slowly, as the darker glosses can be a bit messy. Purse your lips for greater control during application. To add sparkle glitter to the gloss, put a small amount onto the base of your hand and dip the applicator wand in glitter to apply to your lips while still sticky.

Dina shows off her captivating All-Star look.

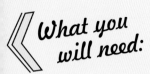

What you will need:

* Rattail brush
* Bobby pins
* Clear rubber band
* Hairspray
* Glitter spray

ALL-STAR HAIR

All-Star hair calls for dramatic styling that may feature a curly ponytail and a high pouf topped off with glitter. All-Star gyms often have a preference for straight or curly ponytails. While both styles look great, curls keep their shape without frizzing out as you jump around, which can help to keep your hair looking neater throughout the performance.

STEP ONE

Start by creating the pouf in front for greater height and front interest. Take a 3-inch section of hair above your forehead and brush it straight up. Use a rattail brush to tease the section; start 2 to 3 inches up and brush down toward the roots. Hairspray the section and let it fall to the side. Brush up the next 3-inch section and repeat (it will take three to four sections). Remember to spray each section once it is teased. When teasing your hair, always work from your forehead back toward where the ponytail will be.

Once teasing is complete, gently comb hair back so that it is lifted in a pouf and smooth on top. Secure the pouf with bobby pins, one on each side. Spray the pouf.

TIP: Use dark bobby pins for brown or black hair and lighter colored pins for blonde or lighter hair so that they are not noticeable.

STEP TWO

Gather hair and use a rattail brush to smooth and brush hair away from your face and up into a high ponytail. Brush down and spray any flyaway hairs. Secure tightly with a rubber band so no strands will fall out. A thicker rubber band will provide more support. Touch up flyaway hairs with hairspray.

STEP THREE

If you wish to have a curly ponytail, use a 1-inch barrel curling iron.

Take a 1x1/2-inch section of hair and spray it. Take your curling iron and, starting at the base to avoid getting kinks in the curls, wrap the hair around the iron and squeeze for about 10 seconds before unwrapping. If curls don't form tightly, use a smaller section of hair. Use hairspray liberally to ensure staying power. Once the entire ponytail has been curled, separate each lock in half to make smaller, tighter, more plentiful curls.

Spenser, age 14

Hair and makeup is different between school cheering and All-Star cheerleading. For All-Star, we put our hair in a big pouf and ponytail, and tease the ponytail as big as we can. For All-Star makeup, we match our team colors, which are lime green and teal. We put sparkly blue eye shadow on the bottom half of the lid and then sparkly lime green all the way up to the brow line and hot pink lip gloss.

For high school, we wear just a pouf and a ponytail with regular makeup and try to look our best.

Spenser cheers for both All-Star and her school and shares her different looks for both.

TIP: Use the highest setting on the curling iron if your hair is natural and healthy. If you have highlights or processed hair, use a lower setting to avoid damaging your hair. Always use caution with irons as they are very hot!

STEP FOUR

Affix a bow. Don't worry about messing up the curls; your hairspray will keep them secure. For extra pizzazz, apply some glitter spray, but remember to cover your face with one hand while you spray.

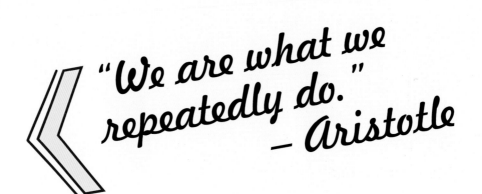

"We are what we repeatedly do."
— Aristotle

NUTRITION, HYDRATION, AND SLEEP

CHAPTER 11

Nutrition

Healthy eating and appropriate weight ranges are priorities for any athlete. Given the additional beauty image that cheerleaders have, coaches and teammates must be watchful that all members of the squad are at a healthy weight. Being underweight or malnourished is not only detrimental to the individual, but it can be dangerous to the squad during stunting. Being overweight also has its drawbacks in performance abilities and increased health risks. Maintaining an ideal body weight and eating healthfully lead to

Shutterstock

good stamina, strong bones, and the ability to focus—not to mention a lifetime of health benefits.

Nutrition at cheer camps is important as well. Most camps serve a substantial lunch, such as a sub sandwich, and allow only water or sports drinks, no sodas. As most camps are held during the summer, it is vital to stay hydrated by taking a drink each time you break.

While the majority of girls realize the importance of good nutrition, it is very difficult to know for sure if someone is eating well. As noted before, it is a safety issue for the entire squad if everyone is not healthy and strong. While the coaches may notice if a girl is too skinny or is not hydrating enough, they will frequently rely on the team captain or individual squad members for inside information. If you feel that another cheerleader may have an eating disorder or is taking drugs or alcohol, notifying the coach is the right thing to do. If a problem is identified or suspected, coaches will notify parents and sometimes the school nurse. Even if it seems scary, it is best for all involved to bring issues out in the open where they can receive proper attention.

Healthy breakfasts, lunches, and dinners that follow the food pyramid are essential to a growing body's development. But these meals are often chosen in advance by parents or schools. Snack time may be the only time you are left to make your own choices. Fresh fruits and vegetables are the best choices because they provide essential vitamins, minerals, and fiber. Fiber is important because it reduces blood cholesterol, slows down sugar absorption, and reduces the risk of developing obesity. However, some prepackaged snacks can still be healthy. When choosing a snack, check that

Ivette, age 17

Nutrition is so important for athletes. I believe in that, my coach believes in that, and my teammates believe in that. I am on the nutrition board with my [school] principals. Another student and I sit down with all the school principals to discuss what's right for the cafeteria, because a good diet is important for everyone at this age. Our bodies are developing and we need to focus on the right nutrition, so when we come to cheer practice we all make sure we are eating right. It's kind of corny—we talk about how the cheerleading team is, and other kids will share about their sports and how they are eating. We get to change around the cafeteria menu based on what we like and what will be beneficial for everyone in the school.

Ivette knows the importance of proper nutrition and works with her school to help all the students make healthy choices.

it contains less than 2 grams of saturated fat, less than or equal to 1 gram of trans fatty acid, and less than 10 grams of sugar per serving.

Don't be fooled by fat-free baked goods—they likely contain significant amounts of sugar, making them no healthier than the original product!

BEST FRUITS AND VEGGIES

Pepper strips
Baby carrots/carrot sticks
Cucumber slices
Broccoli florets
Zucchini slices
Oranges
Pears
Clementines
Grapes
Berries
Celery sticks
Radishes
Unsweetened applesauce
Canned fruit in juice, not syrup

Nutritious food is also delicious. Enjoy fresh fruits and vegetables as satisfying snacks that will help energize your body for cheering. *Shutterstock*

CRACKERS

Cheese crackers
Soup and oyster crackers
Saltine crackers
Wheat crackers
Buttery crackers
Multi-grain crackers

COOKIES

Even cookies can be an OK snack if eaten in moderation. Look for low-fat or fat-free varieties, but remember that a fat-free product is not calorie-free and it is not good to eat more than the recommended serving size. To avoid overeating, take the recommended serving size out of the package and put the package away before you start eating. Some examples:

Graham crackers
Cookie cakes
Butter cookies
Oatmeal raisin cookies

RICE/CORN CAKES

There are many varieties of crunchy and satisfying rice or corn cakes, rang-ing from savory sour cream and onion or cheddar cheese flavors to sweet caramel and chocolate. Look for brands that have the least amount of ingre-dients in addition to the rice or corn for the most healthful, satisfying snack. Topping them with nut butters or fruit increases the protein and fiber while individualizing them to your taste.

PRETZELS AND POPCORN

Most brands of pretzel twists, rods, and nuggets are low in fat but provide a satisfying, salty crunch. Microwave or prepopped popcorn is available in low-fat and flavored varieties.

Hydration

Our bodies are approximately 60 percent water. When we exercise, the water in our bodies maintains an electrolyte (salt) balance and transports nutrients and byproducts to and from cells through the circulatory system. Although we regulate water intake through thirst, the thirsty feeling can't actually keep up with the body's need for water. Since thirst is a poor indica-tor of your body's hydration level, don't wait until you are thirsty to drink. If you wait until you are thirsty to drink, you may already be dehydrated and it will take longer to rehydrate.

What happens if you work out on a hot day, sweating and exerting your-self without replenishing your water? Your blood volume is reduced and your body cannot adequately supply blood flow to the skin and muscles. You begin to show signs of heat exhaustion and may collapse. High humid-ity will add to the risk of heat exhaustion. Symptoms to look out for include pale skin that feels cool and moist, profuse sweating, muscle cramps or pains, feeling faint or dizzy, complaints of headache, weakness, thirst, and nausea, and increased pulse or elevated temperature (greater than 100 degrees Fahrenheit).

Heat exhaustion can lead to serious medical problems, and the best way to avoid it is to keep drinking water. Make sure you take water breaks, and don't be pressured to continue working out if you start to feel weak or display any of the symptoms listed above.

It is good to know that you cannot drink too much water—your body will simply pass the excess as urine.

Sleep

As a teenager and as an athlete, sleep is vital to your health, safety, and abil-ity to balance your life successfully. While everybody has a unique optimal sleep time, the recommended average is between 8 1/2 and more than 9 hours of sleep each night.

There are risks associated with not getting enough sleep, including the increased risk of injury or accident, lower grades and performance in school, problems with moodiness and other emotional and behavioral issues, and increased use of stimulants like caffeine that can make you edgy.

You can self-diagnose a sleep deficit by looking at your mood throughout the day. If you have difficulty waking up in the morning, get irritable or fall asleep during the day, or find yourself sleeping extra long on the weekends, you probably need to be getting more sleep each night.

Many people have trouble getting enough pillow time because they struggle to fall asleep or feel restless during the night. Here are some tips to help you get to sleep on time and sleep through the night:

- Avoid stimulating beverages with caffeine in the afternoon and evening.
- Whether through a nice hot bath or some cozy reading time, spend time relaxing before bed in order to unwind. Avoid watching television or playing with other electronic devices, as they can act as stimulants on your brain.
- Get the light right. Sleep patterns are affected by sunlight, so try to be outside for at least a half hour each day. At night, a darker room will not only help you sleep better, but it will be more restful and healthier for your eyes.
- Set a sleep schedule for yourself. If you fall asleep and wake up around the same time each day, your body regulates itself into the rhythm.

Brienne, age 17

Cheering has really motivated me to improve my time management and my diet so that I can perform without stress and be healthy. Here is how I do it:

I do some homework on the bus ride home. As soon as I get home, I have a quick snack, usually some Wheat Thins crackers with cheese and one or two cookies with some milk. Then it's right back to homework, dinner, and finishing homework. I usually have about twenty minutes to myself to relax before I shower and get to bed. I get ten hours of sleep each night.

I try to eat the right amount of fruits and vegetables (not my favorite!) by getting in a lot of colors: apples, carrots, and salads. Before a game, I'll have pasta for lots of energy. And I drink a lot of water; I drink at least two bottles of water a day.

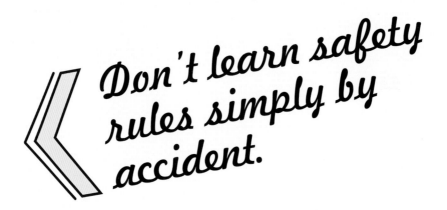

Don't learn safety rules simply by accident.

SAFETY

CHAPTER 12

Shutterstock

IN THIS CHAPTER, we hear firsthand from a sports doctor about putting safety first. We also have reprinted the rules by the American Association of Cheerleading Coaches and Administrators (AACCA) so that you have access to all of the rules and regulations pertaining to the sport. We have also included AACCA guidelines for how individual cheerleaders can make a difference in the overall safety record of the sport of cheering. There are risks in every sports activity. Knowing these risks and being mindful of correct practices can greatly minimize them. Each and every member of the squad must take personal responsibility for her safety and for that of her teammates. Taking responsibility means making yourself knowledgeable whether your coach requires it or not. Seek out best practices. If you're unsure of a skill, don't do it until your questions have been answered. And don't be afraid to speak up when you feel that another squad member may not be performing up to potential. You are not being a tattletale; you are being a responsible teammate.

Safety Rules

The AACCA (American Association of Cheerleading Coaches and Administrators) has published safety guidelines for cheerleaders, as well as a set of guidelines for coaches and administrators. We have reprinted both of these here.

CHEERLEADER'S GUIDE TO SAFETY

These guidelines may be updated periodically. For the latest version, visit http://www.aacca.org

TAKE RESPONSIBILITY

As a cheerleader you are taking part in an incredible athletic activity. You will achieve through hard work and practice. Along with this achievement it is expected that you know your role in safety and risk management, and take every precaution to take care of yourself and your teammates. Though there are many groups and individuals working on your safety, as the athlete safety starts and ends with you.

APPRECIATE THE RISK

The first step in minimizing the risk associated with cheerleading is to have a healthy appreciation for those risks. Cheerleading involves coordinated moves with several other individuals as well as height, inversion, and rotation of the body. Even when properly performed, there is always the risk of having a serious or even fatal injury.

NO COACH, NO PRACTICE

Proper supervision is the key to having a safe environment. If your coach is not present at practice, your team is not to do any building, jumping, or tumbling. Refrain from doing cheerleading skills at home with no adult present and never work on new skills without a qualified instructor present.

BRING YOUR BEST SELF

Your safety and that of others depends on you being at your best and giving your best effort every time. If a basketball player tries a layup at 80%, the worst that can happen is that they don't score two points. That isn't true for cheerleading, and your teammates are relying on you do your part of an intricate stunt. Stay focused mentally on the skill being performed, and commit to the skill fully.

KNOW AND FOLLOW THE CHEERLEADING SAFETY RULES FOR YOUR TEAM

In every level of cheerleading there are rules. These are safety guidelines outlining everything from what you can and cannot wear to what stunts your level of participation allows. Even if you or your team is good enough to do stunts or tumbling sequences beyond those rules, they are in place for your protection. If your coach or team is not following those rules, bring it to their attention or have a parent bring the issue to the attention of the coach, gym owner, or administration.

STAY HEALTHY!

The best things you can do to stay safe are eat well, drink water, get rest, and maintain a strong, healthy, athletic body. When performing an athletic activity the body needs a higher intake of calories and nutrients. It is important to drink plenty of water, to rehydrate what you may lose through sweat. Sleep is the time that the body can heal and rebuild; getting enough sleep helps your muscles and your mind perform better. It is also very important that the body is strong, flexible, and can endure the stress that any athletic activity demands. Conditioning on and off season will help this. Also be careful of "overtraining," where you don't give your body enough rest from athletic activity.

BE AWARE OF YOUR SURROUNDINGS

Before performing any jump, stunt, or tumbling skill, do a quick check to make sure there is enough room to safely perform it, including enough room in the event of a fall. Be sure to only work on equipment (trampolines, tumbletraks, etc.) that is properly supervised by a coach or instructor. Know and follow the surface rules for certain skills like tosses and twisting dismounts.

KNOW YOUR ROLE IN YOUR EMERGENCY ACTION PLAN (EAP)

If your program doesn't have an EAP, get your coach to http://www.aacca. org/eap to get all of the information—or print it out and get it to them yourself! Be familiar with what your role is in the plan and take it seriously; someone's life could depend on it.

DON'T HIDE INJURIES

No one wants to sit out during an injury, but playing through pain could cause an even greater injury down the road that could sideline you for good. It could also cause an injury to a teammate if you aren't able to safely perform your job in a stunt or pyramid. The best thing is to get proper medical attention and rest in order to more quickly return to the team in your best shape.

SPEAK UP!

It can be difficult to speak up to someone in a position of authority, but your safety and the safety of your teammates is at stake. If rules aren't being followed, or if any kind of abuse is happening, let someone know so that it can be addressed. Talk with your coach, parent, school counselor, or any other adult friend that can help get the situation fixed. The angst you feel about speaking up is nothing compared to the feeling you will have if something bad results by not speaking up.

Safety First in Competitive Cheerleading

Dr. Sherry Wulkan

Dr. Sherry Wulkan has dedicated herself to the practice of sports medicine and sees every day the importance of attention to safety and fitness in our sports activities. She is board certified in internal medicine and is a former co-director of Montefiore Hospital's emergency room. Her experiences have covered all types of sporting events, from boxing and UFC to professional tennis (U.S. Open), collegiate swimming and diving, and several international competitions. In this article she gives her unique perspective on how to enjoy cheerleading in a safe and responsible way.

Watch any high school or college cheerleading squad practice today, and you will immediately be impressed by the combination of athleticism and dedication that these young performers have. As cheering has evolved from a motivational activity to a full-fledged athletic event replete with competitions, the risk of injury has become a topic of intense interest and study.

Sprains and strains are the most frequently encountered medical issues for cheerleaders. A sprain is an injury to a ligament, the fibers that hold bones together across a joint. Strains involve muscle and tendon injuries and usually occur when muscles or tendons undergo forceful and unexpected lengthening during contraction.

Proper spotting and support is essential to safety and exemplifies the trust that cheerleaders must feel for their squad members.

Ways to Minimize the Risk of Injury

You've already proven you have what it takes to make the squad, so be proactive about having the knowledge to make it the safest possible season for yourself and your team.

- Recognize when and how most injuries are likely to occur.
- Make sure you are doing everything possible to remain in peak condition.
- Be realistic about your own limitations.
- Make sure you have the appropriate athletic fundamentals to participate in cheerleading.
- Work with a trainer to improve core and back strength and to improve plyometric strength, which is the ability to use your muscles in an explosive way.
- Sometimes the pressure of stepping up can be overwhelming, but if you're insecure in a move, or don't feel in sync with the spotter(s), temporarily eliminate that move from the routine. Work on that maneuver until it becomes instinctive and feels natural so it can be executed properly.

- Don't participate in a practice if you can't focus due to lack of sleep, are distracted by personal issues, or are already injured.
- Take control of your health. Get a comprehensive physical by a sports medicine physician prior to participation.

Many women who compete in events in which they wear figure-revealing outfits diet in an attempt to attain their ideal of the perfect body image. Often young women have unrealistic goals. Although they may superficially appear to be the picture of health, they may medically be older than their age in years.

The clinical athletic triad of amenorrhea (absence of menstruation), osteoporosis (weak bones), and eating disorders plagues many female athletes. Bone demineralization can be especially precarious for gymnasts and cheerleaders, as it increases their risk of fractures.

How can you minimize your risk? Be assertive—take control of your health. If you already have an issue, seek professional advice. Follow these rules to improve your overall health:

- Get enough sleep.
- Ensure that you are consuming the proper number of wholesome calories; reduce the quantity of nutritiously deficient foods whenever possible.
- Make sure you have enough vitamin D and calcium in your diet, as these nutrients may help reduce the chance of fractures.
- Take a good women's multivitamin every day
- Progesterone causes increased ligament laxity; levels of progesterone rise approximately one week prior to onset of your period. As a result, women may have an increased injury rate in the week prior to their period. Try to avoid learning new routines or practicing during this time of the month if you seem to be affected.
- If you do sustain an injury, seek medical attention immediately. In general, the more quickly you get help, the faster you will return to play.

Be proactive about your environment as well. You may wish to enlist your parents' help in obtaining the following information about your coach and school:

- Know who is going to be coaching the squad.
- Find out whether the school requires certification for coaching, the type of certification required, and how frequently certification needs to be updated.
- Determine how many years of experience the coach has in teaching advanced maneuvers such as basket throws.
- Does the facility have emergency plans in place in case of injury?
- Does the practice area have appropriately matted flooring? A foam pit for practicing flips? Would the facility consider matting the area in which you are going to perform during the game (even if outdoors) when possible? The load applied to bone can equal 12 times your body weight during jumping and landing maneuvers (as compared to 2 to 5 times for running). Stress injuries may be easily reduced by regulation flooring.

Modern cheerleading is more dangerous than its predecessor and, if not properly coached, can result in serious injury. Fortunately, safety guidelines have been developed and, with proper preparation, one can minimize risks of injury so that every competitor will have the best opportunity to fulfill lifelong ambitions unhindered by ailments acquired during competition days.

AACCA GUIDELINES FOR COACHES & ADMINISTRATORS

SECTION 1.

GENERAL GUIDELINES

1. Cheerleading squads should be placed under the direction of a qualified and knowledgeable advisor or coach.
2. All practice sessions should be supervised by the coach and held in a location suitable for the activities of cheerleaders (use appropriate mats, avoid excessive noise and distractions, etc.).
3. Advisors/coaches should recognize a squad's particular ability level and should limit the squad's activities accordingly. "Ability level" refers to the squad's talents as a whole and individuals should not be pressed to perform activities until safely perfected.
4. All cheerleaders should receive proper training before attempting any form of cheerleading gymnastics (tumbling, partner stunts, pyramids, and jumps).
5. Professional training in proper spotting techniques should be mandatory for all squads.
6. All cheerleading squads should adopt a comprehensive conditioning and strength building program.
7. All jewelry is prohibited during participation.
8. A structured stretching exercise and flexibility routine should precede and follow all practice sessions, game activities, pep rallies, etc.
9. Tumbling, partner stunts, pyramids, and jumps should be limited to appropriate surfaces.
10. As a general rule, all programs should qualify cheerleaders according to accepted teaching progressions. Appropriate spotting should be used until all performers demonstrate mastery of the skill.
11. Supports, braces, etc., which are hard and unyielding or have rough edges or surfaces, must be appropriately covered. A participant wearing a cast (excluding a properly covered air cast) shall not be involved in stunts, pyramids, tosses, or tumbling.
12. Squad members must wear athletic shoes.
13. When discarding props (signs, etc.) that are made of solid material or have sharp edges/corners, team members must gently toss or place the props so that they are under control.

SECTION 2.

DEFINITIONS

1. Top Person: A person who is held off of the floor by another person or persons.
2. Base: A person who supports the majority of a top person's weight while the top person is off the ground.
3. Spotter: A person who is responsible for assisting or catching the top person in a partner stunt or pyramid. This person cannot be in a position

of providing primary support for a top person but must be in a position to protect the top person coming off of a stunt or pyramid.

4. Post: A person on the performing surface who may assist a top person during a stunt or transition.

5. Bracer: A top person that is supporting another top person in a pyramid.

6. Cradle: A dismount from a partner stunt, pyramid, or toss in which the top person is caught in a face-up, piked position before being placed on the performance area or remounting into another stunt, pyramid, or loading position.

7. Inverted: A body position where the shoulders are below the waist.

8. Loading Position: A position in which the top person is off the ground in continuous movement that puts the bases and top in a position to end the movement in a stunt.

9. Stunt: One or more bases supporting one or more top persons off of the ground.

10. Extended Stunt: A stunt in which the entire body of the top person is extended in an upright position over the base(s). Chairs, torches, flatbacks, and straddle lifts are examples of stunts where the bases' arms are extended overhead, but are NOT considered to be extended stunts since the height of the body of the top person is similar to a shoulder level stunt.

11. Cupie/Awesome: A stunt in which both feet of the top person are in one hand of a base.

12. Double Based Suspended Roll: Dismount with a foot-over-head rotation onto the performance surface or into a cradle.

13. Helicopter Toss: A stunt in which the top person is tossed into the air in a horizontal position and rotates parallel to the ground in the same motion as a helicopter blade.

14. Tension Drop: A dismount from a stunt or pyramid where the top person is directed toward the ground while her feet are held by the base(s) until just before the landing.

15. Knee Drop: Dropping to the knees without first bearing the majority of the weight on the hands or feet.

16. Dive Roll: A forward roll where the feet leave the ground before the hands reach the ground.

17. Basket Toss: A stunt in which a top person is tossed by bases whose hands are interlocked.

18. Elevator/Sponge Toss: A stunt in which the top person loads into an elevator/sponge loading position and is then tossed into the air.

19. Released Pyramid Transition: A pyramid in which the top person in a braced stunt is released from their bases and is in a descending mode before being caught in a cradle, stunt, or loading position prior to being transitioned to another stunt.

20. Hanging Pyramid: A pyramid in which the top person's weight is primarily supported by another top person. Examples of hanging pyramids are: a person being suspended between two shoulder stands; a "whirlybird" stunt where one person's weight is being supported by the legs of a top person in a shoulder sit; and a "diamond head" where two persons are suspended from one shoulder stand.

SECTION 3.

PARTNER STUNTS, PYRAMIDS, AND TOSSES

1. All pyramids and partner stunts are limited to two persons high. "Two high" is defined as the base having at least one foot on the ground.
2. The top person in a partner stunt, pyramid, or transition may not be in an inverted position and cannot transition to another stunt, the ground, or a dismount in an inverted position. Exceptions to this rule are the following:
    1. Double based suspended forward rolls where the top person has continuous hand-to-hand contact with two primary bases or with two posts who are controlling the top person. The top person cannot have contact with one base and one post.
    2. The top person in a stunt may begin in an inverted position on the performing surface and be loaded into a non-inverted position shoulder height or below provided that they have constant contact with a base or spotter until they are in the non-inverted position. A base or additional spotter if necessary must be in a position to protect the head, neck, and shoulder area of the top person.
    3. Suspended splits in a transition are allowed provided there are a total of four bases that support the top person; at least three of the bases must support under the legs of the top person, and the fourth base may support under the legs or make contact with the hands of the top person. Top person must have hand contact with bases during transition.
    4. Partner stunts and pyramids higher than shoulder stand level must have a continuous spotter for each person over shoulder stand level. Spotters are considered part of the squad with regard to the squad member maximum limitation. For single-based extended stunts, the spotter may hold at the ankle of the top person and/or the wrist of the base. If the spotter is supporting under the sole of the foot in any way, they are considered to be a base and would require an additional spotter.
    5. When one person is bracing another (including overlapping of arms), one of the individuals must be at shoulder height or below. Exceptions to this rule are the following:
        1. Extensions (double or single based) may brace other extensions.
        2. Double cupies/awesomes (two cupies/awesomes being held by the same base) are allowed. If the stunt is dismounted to cradles, there must be three people for each top person being cradled. This exception does not include variations such as double heel stretches.
    6. If a person in a partner stunt or pyramid is used as a brace for an extended stunt, that brace must not be supporting a majority of the top person's weight. (To demonstrate this, the foot of the top person's braced leg must be at or above the knee of their supporting leg.)

7. Extended straddle lifts must have an additional spotter for the head and shoulders of the top person (similar position to a double based elevator/extension prep).

8. The bases of any extended stunt must have both feet in direct weight-bearing contact with the performing surface.

9. Hanging pyramids must have a continuous spotter for each shoulder stand involved in suspending another person. Hanging pyramids are not allowed to rotate.

10. In a released pyramid transition the following rules apply:
    1. At least three bases must be under the top person throughout the transition.
    2. Bracers at shoulder level must have a spotter in place during the transition movement. Exception: Shoulder sits and double based thigh stands do not require an additional spotter.
    3. The top person must be in hand/arm to hand/arm contact with at least one bracer during the entire transition.
    4. The top person may not be supporting their weight on any other body part of the person(s) assisting (i.e. shoulders of the bracer).
    5. The top person must be in continuous motion and cannot be supported so that they pause at the top of the transition.

11. Basket tosses, toe pitch tosses, elevator/sponge tosses, or similar tosses are limited to no more than four tossers and must be dismounted to a cradle position by two of the original bases, plus an additional spotter at the head and shoulder area. These tosses may not be directed so that the bases must move to catch the top person. The top person may not hold any objects (poms, signs, etc.) during the toss.

12. Participants may not pass over or under other participants from tosses. There is one exception to this rule:
    1. Single based tosses can go over another person.

13. Free falling flips or swan dives from any type of toss, partner stunt, or pyramid are prohibited.

14. Partner stunts, pyramids, and participants may not pass over, under, or through other partner stunts or pyramids.

15. Single based stunts in which the top person is parallel to the performing surface and the bases' arms are extended must have a continuous spotter at the head and shoulder of the top person (bird, side T, single based flatback, etc.).

16. Multi-based tosses that land in stunts (basket to elevator/extension prep, etc.) are allowed; however, they cannot significantly exceed the height of the intended stunt and cannot include a skill (twist, toe touch, etc.) during the toss. Multi-based tosses cannot land in a loading position. Note: Multi-based tosses that include a skill (twist, toe touch, etc.) must be cradled.

17. A single based toss (one base touching during the toss movement) is allowed into a loading position to that original base.

18. Backward suspended rolls and single based suspended rolls are prohibited.

19. Cradle dismounts from partner stunts or pyramids shoulder height or above require one spotter in addition to the original base(s).

20. Cradle dismounts from partner stunts (other than basket tosses, elevator/sponge tosses, or similar tosses) to another set of bases must be caught by three bases. Any type of gymnastics movement (half-turn, twist, toe touch, etc.) is prohibited.

21. The total number of twists in a dismount from stunts or tosses cannot be greater than two rotations. Exception to this rule:

    1. Side facing stunts and tosses (arabesque, scorpion, kick double full basket, etc.) may add a one-quarter twist in order to cradle to the front.

22. A minimum of two catchers is required when the top person falls away from the bases to a horizontal, flat-body position.

23. Tension drops are prohibited.

24. Helicopter tosses greater than a 180-degree rotation (half-turn) are prohibited. Helicopter tosses require four bases to be in position during the entire release. There must be a base at the head/shoulder area during the initiation of the toss as well as the catch. The bases are not allowed to change positions during the release.

25. Single based split catches are prohibited.

26. The use of mini-trampolines, springboards, spring-assisted floors, or any other height-increasing apparatus is prohibited for competition or performance. These devices may be used for skill development and practice under the supervision of a coach trained in their use.

27. Basket tosses, elevator/sponge tosses, and similar multi-base tosses are prohibited on surfaces other than a mat, grass, or rubberized track.

SECTION 4.

TUMBLING AND JUMPS

1. Dive rolls are prohibited.

2. Flips greater than one rotation are prohibited.

3. Twists greater than one rotation are prohibited.

4. A forward three-quarter flip to the seat or knees is prohibited.

5. Participants may not tumble over, under, or through partner stunts or pyramids, or over or under individuals.

6. Participants may not land in a partner stunt or in a catching position from an aerial tumbling skill. (Example: A back flip from a tumbling pass into a cradle is prohibited; however, rebounding from a back handspring into a cradle is allowed.)

7. Landings for all jumps including knee drops must bear weight on at least one foot. (Example: A toe touch jump or kick to a hurdler position, to the seat, knees, or landing with both feet back, or to a push-up position, is prohibited.)

8. Any type of hurdler position or the position with both feet back (sitting, landing, or lying) is prohibited with the exception of a "Z" sit.

SECTION 5.

SPECIFIC BASKETBALL/INDOOR COURT RESTRICTIONS

The following skills are prohibited at basketball and other athletic contests conducted on courts, except where the area is free of obstructions and non-cheer personnel, and all skills are performed on a matted surface.

1. Basket tosses, elevator/sponge tosses, and other similar multi-based tosses.
2. Partner stunts in which the base uses only one arm to support the top person.
3. Released twists into or from partner stunts.
4. Inverted body positions into partner stunts and pyramids.
5. Twisting tumbling skills.

Copies of these guidelines should be distributed to all squad members and any administrators involved with the cheerleading program. All guidelines should be understood and accepted by all parties involved in the cheerleading program, including advisors, coaches, assistants, squad members, parents, and administrators.

Note: The above safety guidelines are general in nature and are not intended to cover all circumstances. All cheerleading gymnastics, including tumbling, partner stunts, pyramids, and jumps, should be carefully reviewed and supervised by a qualified adult advisor or coach.

Cheerleading jumps, gymnastics, and stunts may involve height and inversion of the body and there is an inherent risk of injury involved with any athletic activity. While the use of these guidelines in coordination with the AACCA Safety Course will help minimize the risk of injury, the American Association of Cheerleading Coaches and Administrators makes no warranties or representations, either expressed or implied, that the above guidelines will prevent injuries to individual participants.

If you have any questions regarding the legality of a specific skill, contact us at 1-800-533-6583.

All content is the property of the American Association of Cheerleading Coaches and Administrators unless otherwise noted. Reproduction without consent is expressly prohibited with the exception of personal use for cheerleading and dance teams.

AACCA
6745 Lenox Center Court, Ste 318
Memphis, TN 38115
800-533-6583

Everyone thinks of changing the world, but no one thinks of changing (them)self.
— Leo Tolstoy

CHARTING PERSONAL GOALS

BEING A CHEERLEADER CAN change your life, and it can also change you. When you begin cheering, there are so many goals to be set, from improving your skills in tumbling and stunts to more personal growth ideals. Sometimes these changes occur over time, and we may not realize how far we have come unless we take the time to record our goals and thoughts along the way. Also, there is something about seeing your goals clearly and in front of you that makes them more real and more attainable. The best way to achieve your goals is to recognize what they are and set them down where you can physically see them. There are a variety of ways in which to do this and different methods may be better for different types of goals.

In this chapter, we will explore some of the methods and how each one can work for you. We will look at best methods of tracking skill goals, motivational goals, and personal goals.

iStockPhoto

Tracking Skill Goals

To keep your goals in front of you, keep a goal sheet for the different skills that you want to conquer. Your sheet will be unique to you based on whether you are a base or a flyer, and whether you have an extensive tumbling background or are a relative newcomer. List all the skills you need and whether they are basic, intermediate, or elite. This way you have a clear visual of your path. Every month, place checkmarks next to those items that you have mastered.

You may wish to do this with a buddy where you allot some time each week to get together and work on a specific goal. Working with a buddy can be helpful because it is fun to have the company and it helps to have someone comment on how you look performing your skill. Are your toes pointed? Do you look confident and remember to smile? Post these goals on a door or a wall where you will see them frequently.

You can also take the squad approach to skill goals. One group made a poster that hangs in the private gym where the squad practices twice a week for choreography, gymnastics, and All-Star type training. The title of the poster is "What Defines Success." Each girl on the squad writes a goal and that day's date on a star-shaped self-adhesive note and sticks it to the poster. When the goal is reached, they write the date they accomplished it on the note so the squad has a visual of their accomplishments.

Many of the goals are about stunts, such as "I want to do a standing tuck" or "I want to be able to get a double out of a stunt," but others are long term, such as "I want to win Nationals."

So whether you keep track of your skills progress solo, with a buddy, or with your squad, you'll always be able to look back on your accomplishments with pride.

Personal Motivation

To keep up the motivation to give your all every day in every way, you need to surround yourself with positive energy and visuals that inspire you to get where you want to be, both in cheering and in life. As stated before, "See it to believe." So make a board or display of the things that inspire you, and put it up in your room where it's the first thing you see in the morning and the last thing you look at each night. The things that motivate people are as varied and individual as people themselves, so don't be afraid to express yourself. The more meaningful the display is to you, the more motivational it will be. The inspirational items may be an old championship ring, a photo of your mom and/or dad, an angel figurine that was a present from grandma, pictures of favorite athletes, or even a big number 10 to symbolize a perfect score.

You can also place reminder goals among your display to give yourself positive energy. When writing your goals, state things in a positive way and don't use any negative words. For example, if you are nervous about an upcoming performance, don't say, "I'm afraid I won't hit my stunt." Instead write a card up that says "I will hit my stunt!" and post it on the display. Positive thinking can make a big difference in your confidence, your performance, and your life.

Always remember that cheering isn't just about stunts, events, and trials—it's about the journey.

Keeping a Diary for Personal Growth

Keeping track of that journey can be very important. You may have a diary that has been given to you as a gift, a small book with a lock and key to record your precious, secret thoughts. You may have filled out a page or two and then abandoned it, or simply written your name in it and then tucked into your bookcase, unused.

Let's shake up your ideas about what a diary is and what it can do for *you*.

Many people keep online blogs as their diaries. While this is a great way to communicate, there is something special about writing content that is meant just for you. There is also something special about using pen and paper rather than a computer keyboard, because it gives your brain time to digest its own output. The results can be magical. The how and what to write will vary from person to person as well as from one day to the next.

"Never discriminate, never omit" is a good rule for diary keeping. The idea is not to write a perfect passage but to bring clarity to your thoughts and help visualize the person you want to be. As mentioned before, you cannot achieve success if you haven't defined what success is. Remember, it's not only about success, but also about the journey there. It is on the journey that we do all of our learning and gather precious experiences. Recording this journey allows us to look back and see how far we have come and grown. It also helps us to internalize those lessons along the way. Sometimes what we are learning is not clear to us at the time; it is only understood in hindsight. Therefore, when recording your thoughts and ideas in your diary, don't leave things out because you think they may not be important enough. You just never know.

Another reason for getting all your thoughts on the page is to help you focus yourself. For example, if you spend 10 minutes (to symbolize a perfect score) each morning putting down your thoughts, then you will effectively have cleared your mind of all the stray ideas and feelings that can get in the way of a focused, productive day. By writing down everything, your mind can

Famous Diarists

Diary styles are as varied as their authors and serve many purposes. Let's look at the ways some famous diarists used this personal time.

LEONARDO DA VINCI

This Italian Renaissance artist and creator wrote in his diary three times every day. Many of his amazing inventions found their start in his diaries, but you need a mirror to read them because he wrote everything upside down and backward!

CHARLES DARWIN

A trained doctor who lived from 1809 to 1882 with an intense curiosity about the natural world, Darwin kept diaries during his travels. These journals incorporated drawings, observations, and even pressed samples of flowers and leaves, and helped him formulate his concept of evolution, which he published in the book *On the Origin of Species*.

SAMUEL PEPYS

A Londoner who lived from 1633 to 1703, Pepys' name is synonymous with diary writing. He filled 3,000 books from the age of 27 to 36, when he stopped due to eyesight problems. His writing, while being entirely personal and not meant for publication, is a unique glimpse into life in his time, as his inspirations were people and details about their lives. While he later became a member of parliament and a naval commander, he is better known as a chronicler of the Plague of 1665, The Great Fire of London in 1666, and the coronation of Charles II.

ANNE FRANK

As a Jewish teenager during World War II, Anne and her family were hiding from the Nazis when she began writing her diary. This famous book has inspired millions and was a source of solace for Anne, who wrote, "The reason for my starting a diary; it is that I have no such real friend."

sort through and prioritize as you go. For example, your morning writing might consist of a list of things you wish to accomplish that day or how you feel before a big game that afternoon. If you choose to spend journal time in the evening, you can get a handle on the events of the day and put them into perspective. For example, you may feel dissatisfied with the way you handled an interaction that day. Writing about what happened and how you feel can help you correct your actions. Maybe you overreacted and need to make amends. Were you really hurt by what was said and need help in confronting the other person? Brushing things under the carpet and hoping they will just go away is not an effective way of managing interpersonal relationships. The best method is to address the issue head on in a calm, collected manner—but only after some reflection to think things through. Once you have sorted through your day and given yourself a game plan for moving forward, you can get a good night's sleep with the feeling that you are in control of your life and are not overwhelmed by events or emotions.

Of course, you may also copy into your diary motivational sayings you come across or add poetry that you found and enjoy or that you wrote yourself. Be creative, be daring, and feel free to express yourself in your for-your-eyes-only journal.

When and what you choose to write is entirely up to you, but try to set aside a particular time for yourself each day. Make writing a priority, and keep this appointment with yourself and your journal until it becomes a habit that you look forward to.

Diary

Shake things up!

Diary

Diary

Sunshine, sand, and spirit!

Diary

Diary

I'm Ready, Teddy, Go!

CHRISTINE
FARINA

AFTERWORD

CHEERLEADING HAS INSPIRED MY life from the moment I first tried out for my high school squad. The feeling of elation when I saw my name posted on the roster is something that remains with me. Cheerleading has widened my horizons by affording me the opportunity to travel as a competitor, coach, and consultant. I've spent many summers on the road working cheer camps and I am always blown away by the energy and enthusiasm that Americans have. I fully believe that if the can-do attitude and positivity of cheerleading were extended into all areas of work and life, the world would be a better place. Teamwork is an often-used term, but how many people really understand what it means to trust in and respect others and work through differences to excel together? Cheerleaders do.

Cheerleading is not simply about attitude, it is also about action. It is about participation and putting yourself out there to make a difference. I often feel that I have the best job in the world. I love getting to know the students and watching them grow and develop into mature adults, helping to shape their lives through the skills and life lessons learned through teamwork and competition. I feel that what I get back from my team is so much more than what I give because I get to do what I love while helping others in a positive environment.

I hope that this book has been informative, but I especially hope that it has been inspirational. I want for you to do your best and give it everything you've got whether you are on the competition floor, cheering for your school team, or simply living each moment to its fullest. As I put this book together, I have been reminded of the rich history of cheerleading and its place in American culture. continue to be inspired by its traditions that are now world renowned. I also applaud the new rules of safety and the focus on personal health through proper nutrition and exercise. These are changes that will impact cheerleaders' lives today and will help provide a healthy baseline to keep you fit and ready for your future.

I have had the honor of winning four National titles as coach of the Hofstra University cheerleading team. All those championship rings are so special to me because they represent the dedication and hard work that went into getting them. I cannot look at them without recalling all the fun and excitement and teamwork that went along with winning them. The rollercoaster ride that comes along with coaching is so worth it. The good days outweigh the bad days and the memories created both in the peaks and in the valleys certainly will remain forever. If I am driving my car or out at an event and Journey's "Don't Stop Believing" comes on, I can't help but take a moment to myself, and to hold on to that feeling that I've been so fortunate to have experienced. When I have a challenging day, the memories my teams have provided give me renewed strength in knowing that with practice and perseverance, I can accomplish anything. Life should be about reaching for the "next best" so I use those rings to keep myself striving and finding new challenges. If you believe you will receive. If you believe you certainly can achieve it all. Life is also about living in the moment. Use these moments in cheerleading to be who you want to be. I hope you will join me in my world of cheerleading!

ACKNOWLEDGMENTS

Christine Farina would like to thank her parents, the Hofstra cheer family, and her husband, Jason, who never stops believing in her.

Courtney A. Clark thanks her boys, Ian and Zachery, and Greg for his love and support.

Special thanks to Hofstra University and the Hofstra cheer team: Angelica Alestra, Ryan Brown, Kevin Brugger, Anthony Chieco, Moet Cordasco-Walsh, Nicole DiSalvo, Jeena Ficcarotta, Monique Hutton, Calison James, Assistant Coach Matt Jones, Alek Kociski, Kelli Mcloughlin, Samantha Montemurro, Jenny Nadraus, Nick Polizzi, Kelly Rancier, Jaclyn Riportella, Arianna Scanlon, Brittany Schoenig, Alexa Sibilio, Alie Sturchio, and Chloe Swain.

Best wishes to all the cheer camp participants from the towns and schools of Bethpage, East Meadow, Freeport, Hauppauge, Holy Trinity, Longwood, Lynbrook, MacArthur, New Canaan, Nutley, Oceanside, Paramus Catholic, Phillipsburg, Rocky Point, Sachem, St. Catharine's Academy, St. Francis Prep, Ursuline, Wall, Walton, and Wayne Valley.

Finally, many thanks go to the following individuals and organizations whose assistance and contributions helped to make this book possible:

Gravity Cheer in Holbrook, New York, especially coach/choreographer Nicole Gabrinowitz and owner Vinny De Marco; Cindy Villarreal and Mason Hughes of Proformance Sports Marketing and Entertainment in Austin, Texas; Dr. Sherry Wulkan of ProHEALTHCare Associates and medical director for the Long Island Sports Care Group (LISCG); Coaches Jamie D'Andrea and Elizabeth Schlitt of Sachem North; David Kirschner of The Spirit Consultants, LLC (www.thespiritconsultants.com); Stephanie Lombardi at Razzle Dazzle Cosmetics (www.razzledazzlecosmetics.com); and Dina DeSimone of LaModa Hair Salon.

INDEX

ABOUT THE AUTHORS

A former competitive cheerleader, **Christine Farina** has been the Head Cheer Coach and Choreographer for Hofstra University's cheer squad since 2003. She has led her team to 5 College National Championship titles and is responsible for clinics and summer camps for cheerleaders of all ages. Selected for her expertise to judge both national and international cheer competitions, she is a well-known and respected member of the cheering community. She has been the Associate Producer for MSG Varsity's hit TV show, "The Cheering Life," and has choreographed halftime routines for the Harlem Globetrotters, New Jersey Nets, and most notably for the 2008 NFL Kickoff featuring the chart-topping recording artist Usher.

As a sports writer, **Courtney A. Clark** brings her experience as a former cheerleader and athlete to her work. Her other books include *Boxing for Beginners*, co-written with Golden Gloves Champion Billy Finegan, and two ghost-written books on golf. She is involved with promoting fitness and sports activities around the country. Photographer Bruce Curtis is a frequent collaborator.

A former Dallas Cowboys cheerleader and entertainment director for the National Football League, **Cindy Villarreal** is now the President of Proformance Sports Marketing and Entertainment, Inc., as well as an agent for Cheer Channel, Inc., a 24-hour online network that showcases content devoted to the world of cheer and dance.

Bruce Curtis has been a professional photographer for many decades, contributing to such esteemed publications as *Time*, *Life*, and *Sports Illustrated*.